Reusing America's Schools

Reusing America's Schools

A Guide for Local Officials,
Developers, Neighborhood Residents,
Planners, and Preservationists

Daniel Carlson

The Preservation Press

National Trust for Historic Preservation

The Preservation Press
National Trust for Historic Preservation
1785 Massachusetts Avenue, N.W.
Washington, D.C. 20036

The National Trust for Historic Preservation in
the United States is the only private, nonprofit
national organization chartered by Congress to
encourage public participation in the preservation of sites, buildings, and objects significant in
American history and culture. Support is provided by membership dues, endowment funds,
contributions, and grants from federal agencies,
including the U.S. Department of the Interior,
under provisions of the National Historic Preservation Act of 1966. The opinions expressed in
this publication do not necessarily reflect the
views or policies of the Interior Department.
For information about memberships, write to
the Trust at the above address.

Printed in the United States of America

5 4 3 2 1 95 94 93 92 91

Library of Congress Cataloging
in Publication Data
Carlson, Daniel L., 1946-

      Reusing America's schools: a guide for
local officials, developers, neighborhood
residents, and preservationists / Daniel
Carlson.

           p.   cm.

      Includes bibliographical references (p.   )

      ISBN 0-89133-184-0

      1. School closings–United States.
2. School facilities–Extended use–United
States. I. National Trust for Historic Preservation in the United States. II. Title.

LB2823.2.C37   1991

371.6' 2–dc20   91-17571

Cover and book design: Allen L. Auvil
Cover photo: Mary Levin
Back cover photos: Keen Development Corporation

Contents

Acknowledgments

Like any undertaking, this guidebook is the result of the support and contributions from many people and organizations. Betty Jane Narver, director of the Institute for Public Policy and Management, backed this project since its inception and gave it a home. The National Trust for Historic Preservation, SAFECO, BP America, and Lorig Associates provided financial support to turn the guidebook idea into reality. The University of Washington, National League of Cities, American Association of School Administrators, National Association of School Boards, and others have enabled the information to be distributed to decision makers and influencers.

Of special note is the personal support through encouragement, review, and suggestions of many persons, especially Bridget Hartman and Lisa Wormser of the National Trust's Critical Issues Fund, Kathryn Burns and Lisbeth Henning of the Trust's Western Regional Office; also Professor Dennis Keating at Cleveland State University, who was present at the conception of the idea and blazed the trail with his own study. Tomas Rodriguez, who found and generously shared with me his unpublished research; Gerald Traub and the Historic Preservation Foundation of North Carolina, Warren Jones, Ben Frerichs, Dan Chasan,

John Curley, Holly Fiala, and Bill Barnes, who lent their advice; the many school district and municipal officials who gave of their time and experience, including: Robert Long, Larry Jacobsen, John Richmond, Harvey Jones, Bill Wilbur, Sherrill Houghton, John Mahaffy, Al Pucci, Rosemarie Bednar, Jerry Rubin, Donna Brown, Janet Van Zandt, Victoria Prinz, Richard Hurlbut, Lynda Rahi, Paul Thiltgen, Ed Talbot, Joe Riedel, the developers both for profit and nonprofit and their professional consultants, including

Bruce Lorig, Bob Kuehn, Harris Hoffman, Dick Valentine, Janet Signor, Renee Berry, Paige Chapel, Les Tonkin, Val Thomas, Robert Burke, Wallace Coffey, Ted Nuncio, Ricanne Hadrian, Tom Kieffer, Mary Powell, Sandy Blovad, Frank McGlone, and Ann Slattery. Lucille Fuller, Dorothy Moritz, and Allen Auvil provided editorial, design, and production assistance, and Bill Grenewald and Buckley Jeppson at The Preservation Press saw fit to help publish the book.

Design detail. The updated exterior of Seattle's Eckstein Community Center plays off Ravenna School's original character.

Photo: ARC Architects, Seattle, Washington

Foreword

A classroom in the Port Costa, California, Elementary School, closed in 1966, appears frozen in time 20 years later.

Photo: Lewis Stewart

In this new guide, Dan Carlson offers a how-to manual for elected officials, school administrators, and neighborhood activists interested in converting schools into centers of community and economic activity. The book is practical in nature highlighting more than 30 instances from around the country where old schools serve new needs from housing to manufacturing, offices to retail stores. Also, the book is concerned with several broader public policy themes as well.

Reusing America's Schools focuses on conversion examples which help achieve public policy goals such as economic development, special populations housing, job training, and historic preservation. It speaks to a new definition of public asset management both within and between school districts and their surrounding municipalities. It asks the reader to rethink our public investments in school facilities to include not only school age populations but, over the course of several generations, all populations.

Sophisticated developers have found that many older schools have a quality of design—high ceilings, floor to ceiling windows, and often sweeping vistas—which make conversion of classrooms to apartments and condominiums extremely attractive. It turns out that typical classroom square footage is the same as a one-bedroom apartment and that turn of the century public policy was to construct school buildings on higher ground to symbolize the importance of education (and thereby assure beautiful views for the future). Is it possible to learn from such examples in Boston, Denver, and Seattle so we can design new schools to serve students today and house elderly residents tomorrow? The answer is "yes" as is recounted in the case of Arvada, Colorado. But why is such planning the exception rather than the rule?

In most communities across the nation the public education function and other governance functions from land use decisions to police protection are separated. But with the institutional separations come barriers to the effective use of a school building and its grounds. Population and economic changes are so rapid today that in some areas, such as the San Francisco peninsula, major high school complexes built to house thousands of students in the 1950s and 1960s were closed a mere 25 to 30 years later due to reduced school age populations. In some states such as California, public law enables municipalities to obtain portions of these sites as community open space at a fraction of the market rate. Municipalities, school districts, and private businesses have forged creative arrangements to use these schools to create community employment, provide parks and community meeting space, and generate revenue for the schools (see the Sunnyvale, San Bruno, and Palo Alto experiences).

In small towns and big cities across the country school closures have been a way of life in the twentieth century. In 1930 there were 260,000 elementary and secondary schools in the United States. By 1960 the num-

Recess circa early twentieth century.

Photo: Seattle Public School Archives

ber had decreased to 116,000 due primarily to consolidation of many smaller elementary schools. Today there are about 85,000 elementary and secondary schools. Often schools have been physically and emotionally situated as an integral part of the community fabric. The preservation of this shared history and community definition can be an extremely compelling public policy act. While the physical meaning of the structure and its impact on the community can be retained, the endeavors housed within may be new and will serve as means of community and economic renewal. The small business incubator center in rural North Carolina, the café,

grocery, post office, and senior housing in northern Minnesota, or the mixed income housing in Boston provide outstanding examples of such rebirth.

Good policy is not the exclusive province of county courthouses and state legislatures. It often begins in the neighborhood or the smallest of towns. When the residents of Jamaica Plain fought gentrification and influenced conversion of the neighborhood school to housing for the homeless rather than condominiums, they were thinking globally and acting locally. When the townsfolk of Port Costa (pop. 250) tried to preserve their old school they ended up changing California state law to allow nonprofits to buy and maintain surplus schools. That is policy from the bottom up. This guide deals with policy issues

through tangible examples. And it offers great hope about America's ingenuity, good instincts, and creativity. The Institute for Public Policy and Management is pleased to publish this work.

Betty Jane Narver, Director
Institute for Public Policy
and Management
University of Washington

Purpose

This guide is intended for several audiences:

■ school officials and managers;

■ elected city officials and administrators;

■ developers and design professionals; and

■ community residents and preservationists.

Each audience has an important role in successfully reusing closed schools and making them contributors to vital communities. The guide concentrates on examples of school conversions that have occurred during the decade 1980-90 and that offer strategies for replication and inspiration. The guide builds upon several excellent sources of information produced during the last 15 years, notably *Surplus School Space: Options and Opportunities*, Educational Facilities Laboratories, 1976; *Surplus Schools In-*

formation Sheet No. 32, National Trust for Historic Preservation, 1982; and *A Guide for the Adaptive Use of Surplus Schools*, Columbus Landmarks Foundation, 1981.

This guide also provides the first comprehensive review of school conversions in the 1980s documenting the financial arrangements and organizational mechanisms employed as federal community development funds dried up. *Reusing America's Schools* emphasizes instances where:

■ leasing arrangements created new development beneficial to the community, generated revenue to the school district, and retained the property in public trust for future school use;

■ noneducational public policy objectives—affordable housing, parks and open space, provision of social services, historic preservation—have been achieved with city governments, nonprofit agencies, developers, and neighborhoods working together;

■ innovative financing and/or mixtures of uses and methods have been employed; and

■ buildings of historic and architectural significance have been preserved and reused.

An underlying precept of the guide is that: "Public schools are one of the major investments taxpayers make in their local communities . . .

they represent a cumulative investment of public tax dollars. It makes sense to maximize the public's return on investment by reusing schools to meet alternative community development needs" (Fiala 1982).

For those readers who have had to close schools and those who may close them in the future, *Reusing America's Schools* contains prosaic as well as unique examples of school building and property conversions. It details the mechanisms of conversion and the steps districts, cities, and developers have taken to reach agreement and to make change. And it outlines the financial terms of a variety of projects so that these approaches may be used singly or in combination as best suited to individual circumstances. In selecting examples, primary emphasis is given to conversions that, because of factors of location, political constraints, or financial feasibility, could not be readily addressed by the private market alone.

One area that the guide does not address is how decisions are made to close a school. Rather, it picks up at the point when the school facility is no longer used to house students and teachers.

This guide can be read through from beginning to end or used as a reference for specific examples of school conversions. To find cases by location, use, or financing and development method, consult the Index beginning on page 64.

9

Choices for Vacant Schools

Throughout the United States, school districts, both urban and suburban, public and private, have been closing school buildings for the past two decades. The National Center for Education Statistics estimates that the number of public buildings in use as schools fell by about 9,000 in that period. The major reasons for this phenomenon have been the decline of the student population, the obsolescence of old school buildings, and, in some localities, court-ordered school desegregation.

After closing schools to reduce operating costs, school boards have five basic choices.

First, they can convert buildings to other functions of the school district (e.g., administration, maintenance equipment storage, preschool education, etc.).

Second, they can lease the building to another public agency or a private business, including nonprofit groups, thus reserving the possibility of reconverting the building to edu-cational use should the need arise. Examples include community centers and social service agencies.

Third, if there is little or no possibility of a future need to reuse the building for educational uses or if the building is too expensive to maintain and operate, school boards may then choose to sell the building.

Applicable law or school board policy may dictate sale by competitive bids through public auction. There may be nonprofit organizations or community development corporations interested in the purchase and adaptive use of closed school facilities. However, these organizations often cannot afford to purchase at a fair market value, however low that might be. Often, sales for a nominal fee to nonprofit purchasers may be allowed, for example, by transfer to the municipality, which in turn transfers title to the nonprofit.

Fourth, if school boards do not wish to lease and cannot find interested purchasers, they can mothball the buildings in the hope that eventually a tenant or purchaser can be found.

Fifth, if either a tenant or purchaser cannot be found or the building is in such poor condition that it constitutes a danger and exposes the school board to possible liability for damages, the most rational option may be demolition. The board can either contract out the job to a demolition contractor and retain ownership of the land itself or it can sell the land and building on condition that the purchaser demolish the building.

The best solutions involve the continuing use of the building either by the schools or through adaptive use. This serves the interests of the schools and the neighborhoods in which the schools are located. Most of the examples cited in this guide are old, historic buildings that are part of the community fabric.

By far, the worst outcome is either an abandoned and deteriorating eyesore or an empty unused lot where a school once stood.

Mothballed schools, especially if they are not properly maintained and secured, become vandalized, are often the locus for crimes such as arson or drug dealing, can depress property values in the adjacent area, and can hurt the reputation of the neighborhood, making revitalization efforts more difficult. Demolition may destroy historic buildings that are architectural landmarks and community anchors. If redevelopment does not occur, the result is a large unused lot which has a very negative effect on the surrounding neighborhood. In either case, instead of being a community asset, the former school or its site becomes a public nuisance.

The Initiators: School Districts That Close Schools

School district elected leaders and managers hold school properties in public trust, foremost as facilities to educate youth, yet simultaneously as substantial community employers and neighborhood centers of activity. The financial plight of many school districts encourages outright sale of underused properties for short-term financial gain. Such a strategy may prove costly in the long term, should increases in school-aged populations require new facilities in the next 10 or 20 years. Replacement costs will be much higher. On the one hand the district is obligated to manage its facilities and property portfolio for maximum efficiency. On the other, it must be concerned about the impacts of its decisions on the larger community's economy, livability, and vitality. Often the school district is ill-equipped or unprepared to conduct property management activities.

The issue of public asset management is complex, and it is not always clear what measures to consider when contemplating a school closure due to declining enrollment. Is the decline in school-aged population a short-term occurrence or a long-term trend? While national statistics indicate a leveling off of school-aged population in the 1980s and a slight increase toward the year 2000, these figures provide little guidance to a school system experiencing precipitous growth or decline. The rapid mobility of families within and among American metropolitan areas also makes facility planning difficult for school districts.

School districts usually initiate action by closing school buildings or selling unused property. Sometimes the actions are dramatic. The Cleveland School Board closed 47 elementary and five secondary schools between 1978 and 1980. In Palo Alto, California, the school district became a land developer, subdivided unused property, and built residential subdivisions to maximize income from its properties. In cities and towns across the country over the past 60 years schools have been closed because of consolidation of rural schools in the first half of the century or the decline of the postwar baby boom starting in the 1960s and 1970s. Several factors conspire to reduce school-age population including low birth rates and gentrification, which tends to raise property values beyond the reach of families with school-age children. But when the number of enrolled students in Cleveland's public schools dropped from 170,000 to 71,000 and Palo Alto's declined from 16,000 to 7,000 (during the period 1970-88), the school districts were forced to act. In California the issue of population decline was exacerbated by the passage of Proposition 13, which reduced property taxes by 50 percent consequently reducing revenue for schools.

Neighborhood Vitality

From a community development standpoint, the adaptive use of a school can achieve many objectives from senior housing to municipal office space, whereas the school board may perceive the surplus building only as a _problem_. Effective school reuse demands decision-making mechanisms that permit the city, school, developers, and local residents to participate in deciding the fate of old schools and to bridge some of the artificial divisions among public agencies with jurisdiction over school properties.

The Reactors: Municipalities and Neighborhoods

Because schools are focal points for neighborhoods and the relationships between families and schools are such emotional issues, closing schools is a decision often deferred by school districts until a crisis is reached and suddenly buildings must be closed, teachers laid off, and neighborhoods impacted.

In Seattle, the school-age population dropped from 100,000 in the early 1960s to 50,000 by the late 1970s when the district announced plans to close up to 20 schools. The city and local communities were not prepared for this and reacted by calling for a broad community study of the impacts of such actions and the options for managing closures. The Joint Advisory Commission on Education, a citizen group advising the city and school district on common educational issues, proposed that the city fund a policy and property management plan. By 1981 a plan was put in place, with a process for cataloging properties for *retention* or *disposal*. Retained schools could be reactivated within one to three years and could be leased for short-term uses. Disposal schools would not be needed in the foreseeable future and could be redeveloped through long-term lease or outright sale.

A property management office was established and a director hired. His background in economic community development with the city of Seattle provided a perspective and professional skill package previously unrepresented in the public school administration. By closing 5 schools in 1978 and 19 more in 1981, Seattle closed nearly a quarter of its school buildings, but because of neighborhood response, city funding, and zoning flexibility, all but 3 school buildings were leased to community and private entities managing the buildings, providing community services, and covering maintenance costs one year later.

In Washington, D.C., as the school district closed buildings, it turned title over to the District of Columbia's public facilities department. The city reacted by leasing some schools to community agencies as emergency shelters, job training centers, and offices. In some cases, the city recommended demolition of old buildings such as the historic Sumner School near the Dupont Circle area of Washington, D.C. (see page 41). The city reacted on a case-by-case basis, using the old schools to provide needed neighborhood services and to house some government functions. By the end of the 1980s, the school district had hired a property manager with plans to recapture many properties from the city for potential development into neighborhood revitalization projects.

Two cities, Boston and Palo Alto, California, offer examples of localities that reacted to closures by developing conscious strategies for the use of closed schools.

Some Generalizations About School Districts and Property Management

■ **School districts see their mission primarily as providing education to children and secondarily as managing the facilities.**

■ **Few districts see themselves in the property management business or have staff capacity to devise and implement short- and long-term asset management strategies.**

■ **If a district has experienced school closures due to declining school age population, closures are viewed as phenomena that have passed and "gone away."**

■ **Rapidly growing districts are giving little thought to future closures or conversion.**

Boston: Affordable Housing

Boston's school department closed 27 schools in 1981. Once declared surplus, control of the properties reverted to the city's department of public facilities. (The Boston school system is technically a city department although administered by a separately elected school committee.) The first city strategy from 1981–84 was to sell surplus properties to private developers at prevailing market rates and to look to the private sector to develop the sites and upgrade the surrounding neighborhoods. School properties in excellent locations were often paired with sites in poorer locations and sold as a package. The strategy had positive and negative consequences. While some beautiful condominiums were constructed, such development had the effect of gentrifying neighborhoods and reducing the stock of affordable housing. Many proposed developments never took place; this was especially true of poorly located sites often in neighborhoods most needing redevelopment. Hence the city found itself with undeveloped, often vacant properties outside its control.

Since 1984 the city has adopted a different policy toward old school buildings: conversion to mixed income housing with deed restrictions and ownership structures that increase the city's stock of affordable housing. From 1984 to 1989, a total of 12 former schools has been converted to 472 housing units, 60 percent of them occupied by low- and moderate-income residents. Half

the schools were developed by non-profit housing developers including neighborhood development corporations.

The city accomplished its policy of providing affordable housing through several actions:

■ discounting the sale price of properties;

■ using local, state, and federal funding programs to subsidize development;

■ involving community-based non-profit organizations in joint ventures and syndications with experienced developers and investors; and

■ conditioning sale and lease agreements obligating developers to provide affordable or special needs housing.

An important factor in the Boston experience is that the city was empowered to pursue its policy without confronting a separate school district whose objective was to maximize return from the sale of its properties. The city made a decision to fund affordable housing and forego potential revenue from school property sales.

Another feature of the Boston experience is the conversion of the public facilities department from an agency that disposed of surplus properties to an agency that developed surplus properties into affordable and special needs housing. New personnel were hired to work with neighborhoods, community development corporations (CDCs), nonprofit and profit-making developers and other agencies to create school reuse deals. This special expertise was nurtured by recruiting personnel from CDCs

and staff with housing and social service backgrounds (see pages 26, 53 and 56 for details on Bowditch, Sumner Hill House, and Leen schools).

Palo Alto: Open Space, Community Centers, and Child Care

This city of 55,000 in the South San Francisco Bay area was drawn into issues specific to the closure of Terman Middle School in 1978. Following state law, the school board appointed a property advisory committee to review options for the disposition of the facility. Its recommendation was to retain the structure as a community center, a portion of the grounds as public recreation space, and the remainder as publicly assisted multifamily housing. A neighborhood coalition formed to oppose the plan. In 1980 the city council adopted the community center-housing concept and established a mechanism to resolve the neighborhood conflict. A working group composed of elected and appointed representatives was formed and provided a budget to hire an architect to formulate a plan and reach agreement. To assist the process, a facilitator was hired. In a year's time an agreement was reached and the city and school district entered into a lease purchase agreement (see page 51 for complete details of the case).

But no sooner had this success been achieved than the Palo Alto Unified School District (PAUSD) approached the city for permits to begin demolition and residential lot subdivision on other school sites. It was becoming clear that PAUSD's aggressive effort to maximize the value of its assets was going to increase residential density in a city that was attempting to preserve open space and areas for community use. The city reacted by examining the broader issue of city and school district interrelations.

A first step was creation of the City-School Liaison Committee to encourage discussion between city and elected school officials. The committee comprises two city council and two school board members. Its powers are advisory; the full council and school board must vote to approve all matters. The committee's purpose is to plan and negotiate proposals regarding school site development and the financial and policy arrangements inherent in surplus school issues.

A second step was a formal recognition by the city government of the important interplay of city government and school districts in retaining healthy communities and schools. Through a resolution the city council committed itself to

■ integrate school sites into the community;

■ offset financial problems of the school district;

■ invest in future education of youth; and

■ establish ways for the city and school district to work together on a continuing basis.

A third step was a commitment to lease surplus school properties for community use and to include with the lease a covenant that the school district properties could not be developed during a specified period. This "Lease and Covenant Not to Develop" became effective in 1990. Its term is 15 years with one 10-year and one 5-year renewal option. In the first year the city will pay a total of $4 million to the school district, which provides PAUSD the funds it needs to balance its budget. Under the lease the city pays $2.7 million for lease of the 35-acre former Cubberly High School site, which contains 20 buildings including a theater, pavilion, gymnasia, classrooms, and recreational fields. The Cubberly site will be managed by the city as the primary home of community arts, performance, and educational organizations. The city pays $1 million for the school district not to subdivide or develop six properties "in order to prevent a further

burden on the city's infrastructure and in order to preserve a substantial amount of the city's remaining open space." Finally the city pays $300,000 for the lease of space in 11 open schools to operate before and after school day care.

The fourth step was the proposal to fund the city-school arrangement with a new tax on the city-owned utilities. Voters approved the tax.

The process has not been without difficulties. Just as the City-School Liaison Committee had reached agreement on which schools would be closed and covered by the lease and covenant, a new school administration decided to change the list of schools, and negotiations had to begin anew. Further, most communities are not as affluent as Palo Alto. But the process, the mechanisms, and the local funding used here can enable city and school district cooperation to occur in any community in order to address future situations.

A statement of neglect—a boarded-up school attracts graffiti and vandalism. This is Cleveland's Hodge School before conversion to artists' housing.

Photo: Novus Architects

Zoning and Land Use

While school districts typically own the surplus school property, the city or county has authority over the uses to which the property can be put. Therefore, review of existing zoning is essential to understanding the future options for a site and for determining its value to the district and community. Proper zoning is vital in order to reach a consensus among the district, the developer, and the neighborhood. Depending on the case, the district may apply for a zoning change or the developer might be the applicant.

In Seattle, the city and school district have created the School Use Advisory Committee (SUAC). A SUAC is formed for each school declared surplus by the district. Its purpose is to review options for conversion and recommend appropriate uses including necessary zoning changes.

SUAC is formed by the city's Department of Community Development to whom it issues its report, which is then transmitted to the city's Department of Construction and Land Use, the zoning administration agency.

Seattle's School Use Advisory Committee (SUAC)

What is a SUAC?

A School Use Advisory Committee (SUAC) is a seven-member body that may authorize a zoning use not otherwise permitted within an existing or former public school building. A SUAC is formed for each school that the Seattle School District proposes for uses that are not authorized under present zoning. The school district initiates this process by applying to the city's Department of Construction and Land Use (DCLU) for a special exception to the zoning code. The Department of Community Development (DCD) then begins formation of a SUAC for each school building. The committee's role is to hold public meetings and to recommend conditions and uses that will be permitted in each building.

Who are SUAC members?

Each SUAC consists of the following members:

■ a representative from DCD to serve as chairperson; a representative from the school district or current building owner;

■ two persons residing within 300 feet of the school site selected in cooperation with the community organization that represents the area;

■ a representative of the parent-teachers group or, in the case of a closed building, a representative of the neighborhood;

■ a representative from the Joint Advisory Commission on Education (JACE); and a nonvoting representative from DCLU to provide technical zoning assistance.

What is the SUAC process?

It conducts a minimum of three public meetings in a 90-day period.

It gathers and evaluates public input.

It develops recommended uses for the school building and ground and use criteria (conditions to protect surrounding neighborhood).

It transmits recommendations to DCD director.

What is the process for decision making?

DCD director establishes final uses and criteria for school buildings and grounds.

If appealed, the hearing examiner processes appeal and rules on criteria and uses.

DCLU uses criteria to issue or deny use permit applications.

A surplus school request to rezone carries great weight when recommended by the SUAC. Conversely, a request to rezone without SUAC support would stand little chance of success in Seattle.

In Boston, school conversion proposals are presented by the public facilities department to the subplanning and zoning advisory committees. These subcommittees are appointed by elected neighborhood councils. They have advisory power regarding zoning.

In San Francisco, the school district works closely with the city planning staff to determine proper zoning, development guidelines, and design guidelines for properties it wishes to see developed. In several cases, the district has applied for zoning reclassification itself because:

■ consultants and advisors believe the district will receive more money when leasing a properly zoned prop-

erty, and the district will have greater success than a developer in obtaining the rezone; and

■ developers want new zoning in place before bidding on a property lease.

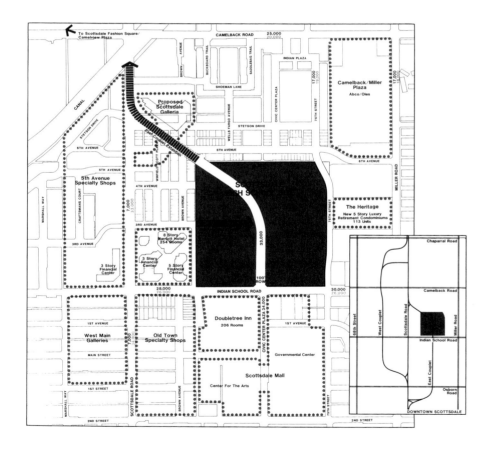

The city and school board of Scottsdale, Arizona, carefully detailed the siting and zoning characteristics of the surplus high school campus in a prospectus for developers.

Planning for Sale or Lease

School districts and other entities, such as cities and counties, must take stock of the properties, the locations, future needs, and a variety of other factors, and then decide whether to sell or lease surplus properties. Perhaps more accurately, the determining body must decide which property to sell or lease. California requires each of its 1,043 school districts to have a property advisory committee, which works with staff to prepare a facilities plan and any recommendations to sell or lease specific properties to the school board.

Many factors must be considered in developing such a facilities management and asset management plan. These include the age and condition of existing buildings, their importance to the surrounding neighborhoods, the location and potential for conversion to various uses, demographic projections of school-age population in the short, medium, and long term, and the correspond-ing likelihood of needing educational facilities to house students in a given location in the future. Such a plan requires periodic revision and often benefits from the assistance of specialized professionals, including

- real estate economists to ascertain land value and development trends;

- appraisers to accurately value the properties and provide the basis for sale or lease pricing and negotiations;

- demographers to project population trends; and

- developers who understand risk assessment and financing requirements.

Selling a surplus school property has the following advantages:

- it is a one-time simple process;

- the school district obtains cash immediately;

- there is no need for a school district staff to manage property; and

- it may be the only practical way to dispose of a given property.

Leasing surplus property has the following advantages:

- it provides a long-term income stream to the district;

- it retains the land in public control, guaranteeing interim use and making it available for future use;

- it can maximize revenue to the district over time; and

- it can offer greater flexibility to the developer and the district in use of property and revenue.

It is often desirable in long-term leases to sell the building and lease the ground. One real estate consultant states it very simply: "Don't ever sell dirt." Leases are most feasible in communities experiencing growth and healthy economic conditions. In communities struggling with economic development, it may be difficult to hold on to a vacant piece of property, because it is not certain that the future will bring increased value. Also, present conditions are perceived as equivalent to the disintegration of neighborhood and community.

In **Daly City, California**, a middle class suburb south of San Francisco, the Jefferson High School District closed Serramonte High School in 1981. The district, which serves several coastal communities on the San Francisco peninsula, had experienced dramatic enrollment declines. The school board debated sale versus lease of the 38-acre property. Its decision was assisted by state law that requires revenue from sales to be applied to either maintenance or new construction capital needs. However, lease revenue can go directly to the general operating budget. Since the district wanted the most control over its revenue, it opted to lease a portion of the Serramonte site.

The property was divided into a first parcel of 18 acres, including the school buildings, and a second of 20 acres. The 20-acre parcel was leased to a developer for market-rate housing development and a medical office building. Jefferson High School District receives $1 million annually from the base lease. The agreement calls for yearly increases of $50,000 for 25 years at which time the terms of the lease are reevaluated. The long-term lease is for 99 years.

The 18-acre site now houses the district's administrative headquarters as well as rental space for community agencies, including day care and social service providers.

In **Boston** both lease and sale arrangements further goals of affordable housing. Jamaica Plain High School was converted into 75 housing units (see page 53 for details). The land was leased to a community land trust on a long-term lease. The trust is comprised of the Jamaica Plain Neighborhood Development Corporation and the Sumner Hill neighborhood association. The trust is dedicated to the land's use as housing and assures that neighborhood concerns and needs are met. The building was sold to the trust by the city's public facilities department for $1 and then leased to a private developer with whom the trust has a profit-sharing arrangement.

Older schools add special character to their community
Photo: Lewis Stewart

State and County Incentives to Leasing

In the 1970s California state policy discouraged school districts from active involvement in property management under the belief that districts should concentrate on educating. Lease revenues could only be used for deferred maintenance and capital improvements. In the early 1980s this policy changed to encourage local districts to manage properties in order to generate revenue from sources other than the state.

In King County, Washington, the large urban county encompassing Seattle, the zoning code specifically permits a wide range of uses for surplus schools retained and leased by districts. Included are housing and social services not otherwise allowed in the underlying zoning. However, school properties sold by a district are subject to the underlying zoning of the site. Zoning regulations encourage districts to retain properties for future school use and for interim community uses.

In **Arlington County, Virginia**, a land trade was used to relocate a sheltered workshop in a closed school (see page 60). The Sheltered Occupational Workshop of Northern Virginia operated a printing and binding facility on a cramped site near a new subway station. The county wanted the property. The county obtained title to a closed school with commercial zoning from the school board, helped obtain a use permit, and provided $350,000 in Community Development Block Grant funds for renovation. In turn, the sheltered workshop relinquished title to its old facility to the county.

Leasing holds the advantages of providing a revenue stream to the school district while simultaneously keeping the land in public trust. It offers private sector opportunities for profit while providing needed community services and revitalization. Leasing revenue can be minimal, covering basic maintenance and operation of the building, or as much as the $2 million dollars the Fremont Union High School District nets annually from the lease of the closed Sunnyvale High School to Westinghouse Corporation as an engineering center (see page 40).

Five Inspirational School Conversions

Of the more than 30 school conversion cases highlighted in this guidebook, five stand out as representative of the kind of creativity and problem solving which can turn a closed school into a focus of community revitalization and, in the process, generate revenue for the school district and the developer. The inspirational five described here represent locations across the country: the San Francisco Bay area, Cleveland, Boston, Denver, and Seattle; three of the conversions are leases, and two are sales.

■ **Pen/Crest Center**—a mixed educational, business, nonprofit, megacourtroom, and recreation center in a former high school campus in San Bruno, a small city south of San Francisco;

■ **Hodge School**—a former elementary school converted to artists' housing by a neighborhood development corporation in Cleveland;

■ **Bowditch School**—a historic elementary school building converted to housing for the formerly homeless in Boston;

■ **Capitol Hill Senior Resource Center**—a comprehensive health and social services complex in the oldest school in Denver; and

■ **Wallingford Center**—a mixed retail and moderate-income housing development in Seattle.

Pen/Crest Center and Bowditch deal with resolving community conflict. When San Mateo Unified High School District closed Crestmoor High School, the residents of San Bruno were not in favor. The district's first proposed sale to the postal service as a computer center caused further community resentment. Then the district changed strategies and embraced the property management role that led to a successful deal with the city leaders: the track and recreation fields would be leased to the city for $1; in return

the district obtained a master use permit to lease space to local businesses and nonprofits in the new Pen/Crest Center.

Bowditch School was sold by the city of Boston to developers to be converted to artists' housing. That proposal failed and was replaced by plans for condominiums. Vocal opposition and court challenges by factions of the surrounding community ensued claiming that the real need was for affordable housing. To break this impasse, the city asked a respected nonprofit developer of housing for the homeless to consider the site as a project. The local state assemblyman was enlisted to mediate between community factions opposing and supporting homeless housing. The school, with use restrictions

The grand scale of an arched window waits at a stair landing.

Photo: Tonkin/Koch Architects

conveyed with the title, was sold to the nonprofit development group, which turned to its financial adviser for a bold syndication plan based on low-income housing and historic rehabilitation tax credits. The result is 45 units of housing in a historically significant building.

The Hodge School and Capitol Hill Senior Resources Center are examples of nonprofit organizations successfully becoming developers. The St. Clair-Superior Coalition, concerned about threats to its working class and racially and ethnically mixed area, sought to redevelop one of several closed schools in its community (the others had been vandal-

ized and one destroyed by fire). Foundation grants, bank loans, and predevelopment funds from the Local Initiatives Support Corporation (LISC) were obtained and a plan to develop artists' housing was created. The city and school district cooperated in turning title over to the neighborhood association. Thirty-seven units of artists' housing not requiring rent subsidy were occupied at the opening in 1990.

Capitol Hill Senior Resources Center was the brainchild of two physicians, themselves advanced in years, premised on the idea that such a center

could assist people to live independently in the Capitol Hill community of Denver. They formed a nonprofit organization and responded to a school district Request for Proposal (RFP) for the sale and development of Emerson School, the city's oldest. Their bid of $400,000 was not the highest but was accepted by the school district, which structured a 16-year purchase schedule enabling the deal to work. An unwitting ally in the deal was the high bidder who proposed conversion to an adult entertainment complex.

Wallingford Center in Seattle has revitalized a commercial street in a middle class neighborhood through creation of shops and restaurants at the street level in the closed Interlake school. The city worked with the local chamber of commerce and community council to develop an RFP and select the developer. As with Bowditch and Hodge, city funding made it possible for the developer to carry out the project. The project became feasible when HUD funds, available through the city, were applied to 24 apartments on the top floor. The school district sold the building to the private developer. The land is leased for 99 years. The school district receives $96,000 annually plus 25 percent of net profit from the project in lease payments.

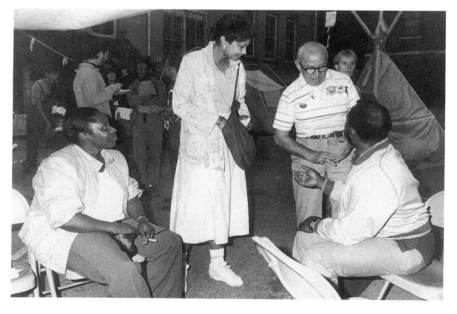

Activists erected a tent city to protest Boston's plans to sell the closed Bowditch School for a condominium development rather than affordable housing.

Photo: City Life

The nonprofit developers of the Bowditch and Hodge schools were successful in putting together development teams of financial advisers and strategists, architects, construction managers, property managers, attorneys, and accountants.

Pen/Crest Center, San Bruno, California

Current Use: Mixed educational, business, nonprofit, court system, and recreation.

Original Use: Crestmoor High School, built in 1962.

Description: The San Mateo Union High School District serves six San Francisco Peninsula cities: San Mateo, San Bruno, Hillsborough, Millbrae, Burlingame, and Foster City. From a high point in the mid-1970s the district's enrollment declined from 12,000 to about 7,500 students in 1980 when Crestmoor High School was closed. The school, consisting of six buildings, each approximately 20,000 square feet, is sited on 40 acres in a residential area in the hills of this primarily middle class city. A generic campus layout was designed for the district in the 1950s and employed in four high schools. Representative of an industrial type design, one-story classroom buildings are interconnected by covered walkways enclosing courtyards. Steel I-beams define the typical classroom size of 28 by 28 feet. Metal walls were designed to be movable and to configure into new spaces. The terraced hilltop site provides vertical variation to the campus with the theater and gymnasia on a lower grade than other buildings. Two pools and a courtyard are contained in the layout. A track, recreation fields, and parking area complete the site.

Today the mixed-use campus is managed by the school district and is occupied by 58-tenant organizations ranging from day care programs to a superior court trial facility to a catering service. It is part incubator business center, part educational facility, and part law offices. As John Mahaffy, the district's director of financial services boasts, "We can marry you, hold the reception, and, if it doesn't work out, we can divorce you all at Pen/Crest Center."

Tenants of the center include:

■ Peninsula High School, the district's 240-student continuation high school, with, among others, students who have dropped out of other schools, been on probation, or represent special circumstances such as school-age mothers;

Crestmoor High School [top] was built in 1962 and closed in 1980. The gymnasia were converted into a sophisticated court facility [above] complete with a computer room for processing information in complex trials.

Photo: David Carlson

- small businesses, such as a specialty food firm, acupuncturist, insurance agent, children's gymnastics school, and a computer services company;

- A mega-courtroom designed to accommodate hundreds of attorneys at one time at 24 separate tables (each connected electronically to the judge's desk), judge's chambers, jury room, support staff rooms, and a computer room enabling high speed processing of information during complex trials and hearings. The courtroom was converted from the theater and a portion of one of the gyms;

- nonprofit service providers including county-funded head start and special education programs, and YMCA preschool and day care;

- two churches; and

- law offices, built to specifications including armored telephone cables to protect against bugging, and a shower facility for after-track workouts.

Development Process: In 1982 the school district conducted a process to determine which high school would be closed. Crestmoor was the choice. The decision caused great resentment in San Bruno and may explain a five to zero city council vote opposing a school district plan to sell the closed site to the United

States Postal Service as a computer center. The school sat vacant and was vandalized. (A student drove a bulldozer through the concrete block and steel wall of the gymnasium clear across the wood floor until the "Cat" lost traction at the bleachers on the far side!)

Arrival of a new superintendent in 1984 helped change the political climate concerning the facility and led to an agreement between the city of San Bruno and the school district. The district agreed to lease the athletic fields to San Bruno for $1; the city issued a master use permit, which allowed the district to rent and lease space in the old school

Entrepreneurship in Education and Property Management

Pen/Crest's Ridgeview Room

The attractive brochure produced by the San Mateo Union High School District describes the Ridgeview Room: "A 1,600 square foot meeting room overlooking the beautiful rolling hills of San Bruno providing the perfect setting for your staff meeting, networking meeting, or any other get-together." Former classroom space has been carpeted and converted to a meeting room with catering service.

While not unique to a hotel or restaurant, such dining and meeting services are not the usual fare for school districts. Yet this "bridge be-

tween business and education" has proven so successful that a second Ridgeview Room has just been opened.

Here's how it works: The school district maintains and reserves space through the Pen/Crest rental office. The district cosponsors the food service in partnership with a private gourmet food service business, named Select Fresh Fine Foods, which is a Pen/Center tenant. High school students enrolled in the Food Education and Service Training (FEAST) program prepare and serve the food (thereby meeting the program objective of providing instruction in preparation and attractive presentation of fine foods leading to careers in the food preparation and marketing industry). Select Fresh

Fine Foods provides the foodstuffs and offers the training opportunities. The Clarion Hotel in Millbrae donates valuable business advice to the project.

An advisory committee made up of school district representatives from the board, superintendent, principals, the county, city mayor and council, service clubs, hotels and caterers oversee the Ridgeview Room endeavor. The project meets a community need, generates revenue, enhances an educational program, and fosters relations among the district, business leaders, and local officials. Initial investment costs were low and the returns are high.

building to the wide variety of tenants without applying for a use permit on a case-by-case basis.

The district began active management of the site by moving Peninsula High to Crestmoor along with other programs. These ranged from special programs for mentally and physically disturbed youth to a Food Education and Service Training (FEAST) program. Community organizations also rented space. A big break came in 1987 when a judge in the Superior Court of San Mateo County was selected to preside over a large and technically complex trial of national consequence. The case involved environmental damage caused by Shell Oil Company at the Rocky Mountain Flats site in Colorado and required courtroom seating and other facilities to accommodate hundreds of attorneys and expert witnesses from around the world. The physical requirements exceeded most court systems' capabilities.

The San Mateo County Court system approached the school district and inquired about use of a portion of the Crestmoor site. Would the district undertake tenant improvements to convert the theater into a high-tech courtroom? And would it construct legal office space for the firms that would establish on-site branches for the duration of the multiyear trial? The district agreed to make the modifications and lease the space to the superior court and attorneys wishing to locate on-site. The Shell Oil trial ended in 1988. In 1989 the courtroom became the location for hearings on State Proposition 103, which established new regulations and limits on auto insurance in California.

Terms of the Deal: The San Mateo Union High School District is the owner and manager of the property. It has an on-site property manager and a rental and lease office. Rents average 50¢ to 60¢ per square foot compared to 80¢ to 90¢ per square foot in commercial areas of San Bruno. Net revenue generated annually is $200,000 ($300,000 during the Shell trial). As landlord, the district maintains the physical plant and parking. The athletic fields are maintained by the city of San Bruno under terms of its five-year lease. Rentals for court use are on a month-to-month basis. Costs of major property improvements such as court renovation are borne by the tenant.

Owner: San Mateo Union High School District
650 North Delaware Street
San Mateo, California 94401
John Mahaffy, Director of Fiscal Services
(415) 348-8834

Contact: Kathy McNeil
Pen/Crest Center Rentals and Leases
300 Piedmont Avenue
San Bruno, California 94066
(415) 583-4293

Hodge School, Cleveland, Ohio

Current Use: Artists' housing and workspace.

Original Use: Hodge Elementary School, built in 1905 and closed in 1980.

Description: Hodge School was originally constructed in 1905 with additions built in 1911 and 1912. Designed by noted Cleveland public school architect Frank Barnum, the main building has two stories of masonry construction around steel beams, making the building virtually fireproof. Floor-to-ceiling classroom windows plus a series of skylights and areas of glass brick floors provide abundant natural light to the interior. The total floor area of the three structures, located on a two-acre site, is nearly 44,000 square feet.

Hodge School is located in the St. Clair-Superior neighborhood of Cleveland in a residential area several blocks from the main commercial thoroughfare. The St. Clair-Superior neighborhood is multiracial. Its northern industrial tier borders on Lake Erie. Its residential areas are now adjacent to predominantly black neighborhoods to the east and south. Its population, employment, and services have declined since the 1960s, a phenomenon that applies to most Cleveland neighborhoods.

The St. Clair-Superior Coalition, a community-based advocacy organization, has converted the school into a total of 38 rental living/workspaces

The Hodge School before the
St. Clair-Superior Coalition
redeveloped it.

Photo: Novus Architects

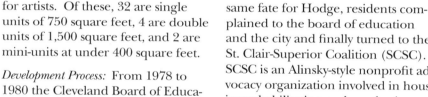

for artists. Of these, 32 are single units of 750 square feet, 4 are double units of 1,500 square feet, and 2 are mini-units at under 400 square feet.

Development Process: From 1978 to 1980 the Cleveland Board of Education closed a total of 47 elementary and 5 secondary schools. The Hodge School and two others in the St. Clair-Superior neighborhood were part of this closure episode. Residents were concerned about having boarded-up buildings in the area with the attendant threats of vandalism, loitering, and reduced property values. One of the closed schools, Sowinski, was repeatedly vandalized and burned by arsonists, resulting in its demolition in 1985. Fearing the same fate for Hodge, residents complained to the board of education and the city and finally turned to the St. Clair-Superior Coalition (SCSC). SCSC is an Alinsky-style nonprofit advocacy organization involved in housing rehabilitation and weatherization, utility rates, arson, street crime, and employment.

In 1985 SCSC formed a Hodge School Redevelopment Committee of 20 residents to determine if the school should be redeveloped or torn down. A survey of 300 surrounding residents indicated a majority preference for redevelopment into day care and senior citizens' services.

In 1986 SCSC obtained funding from two local banks to conduct a feasibility study of Hodge. The consultant found the buildings to be structurally sound and recommended a two-stage development. In the first phase the two annexes were to be rehabilitated for an anchor day care tenant. In the second phase the main building was to be remodeled as a mixed-use complex for commercial use, office space, and social services. The project was estimated to cost from $1 million to $1.2 million.

SCSC had no capacity and no experience in development or construction. They did, however, have a more supportive environment in which to attempt economic development activities than at the time of Hodge's closure. By the mid-1980s the Local Initiative Support Corporation (LISC), city of Cleveland, Ameritrust Development Bank, and several foundations were interested in supporting neighborhood-based economic development. With expressions of interest totaling $1.2 million from these sources, SCSC Executive Director Renee Berry took the first step and sought a co-developer with experience and capital.

A potential partner appeared in the form of a major construction firm, but subsequent negotiations failed for a basic reason: the proposed redevelopment of Hodge School would not yield market rates of return.

By 1988 SCSC decided to develop Hodge School on its own, not as day care and social services, but as artists' housing with studio workspace. Berry defined the concept and conducted market surveys of artists, warehouse and loft owners, and real estate agents to understand demand for artist space. She placed ads in newspapers and artists' networks announcing availability of housing and received more than 60 inquiries. To assist in turning this new strategy into a fundable business proposition, LISC retained predevelopment consultants for SCSC. One consultant, Shorebank Advisory Services, was able to refine the pro formas for the project, prepare cash flow projections, and critique materials before submission to the lending institutions. The other consultant (an individual) provided estimated costs of construction and rehabilitation services and served as project manager during the development phase.

The city of Cleveland's Economic Development Department saw the project as a means of revitalizing a deteriorated neighborhood and made funds available for artists' housing and for housing rehabilitation and repair in the surrounding neighborhood. City Councilman Gus Frango, who represented the district, endorsed the project. The Cleveland School Board agreed to transfer title to the city without requiring other land in return.

The lending institutions were convinced by the business plan that a market existed for artists' housing and that loans would be repaid from rental revenue.

Terms of the Deal: Title to the property transferred from the school board to the city and then to Hodge Ventures, Inc., a wholly owned, profit-making subsidiary of St. Clair-Superior Coalition, which was to develop, own, and manage the facility.

Total project cost for the Hodge School Artist Housing was $1.2 million. Of particular significance was that funding for the project included no rental or operating subsidy.

Rents ranging from $100 to $450 per month were projected to cover operating and financing costs. A combination of conventional and reduced-rate loans along with recoverable and outright grants made up the financing package. This included mortgages of $245,000 from Ameritrust Development Bank, $175,000 at 6 percent from LISC, and $100,000 at 3 percent from the Cleveland Foundation, all payable in 10 years.

The city of Cleveland made two loans, a $200,000 Neighborhood Development Impact Grant for $170,000 for 25 years at 0 percent and $150,000 from the Small Business Revolving Loan Fund. Foundation and government grants added $440,000 to the package.

Owner: The St. Clair-Superior Coalition
6408 St. Clair Avenue
Cleveland, Ohio 44103
Renee Berry, Executive Director
(216) 881-0644

Development Consultant:
Shorebank Advisory Services
1950 East 71st Street
Chicago, Illinois 60649
(312) 288-0066

One of 38 rental living/workspaces for artists in the former Hodge School. This project brings new life to an old neighborhood while increasing the stock of affordable housing.

Photo: Novus Architects

Bowditch School, Boston, Massachusetts

Current Use: Single room occupancy (SRO) housing for formerly homeless people.

Original Use: Bowditch Elementary School, built in 1892.

Description: Closed in 1981, this three-story stone structure in a racially and economically mixed Boston neighborhood has been renovated to retain historical landmark status. Original wainscoting and hardwood floors remain as does the unique system of two sets of double sash windows, designed to insulate during the winter. This renovated school is now a lodging house consisting of 30 SRO units and 6 apartments accommodating 45 residents who share one central characteristic: they are all formerly homeless.

The top floor has been converted into 7 apartments: 3 three-bedrooms and 3 two-bedrooms, plus a two-bedroom residence for a live-in manager. On the second floor, 4 classrooms have been converted into 16 SROs, each cluster of four rooms sharing a bath, as well as another two-bedroom live-in manager's residence and a large hall that serves as a common living room and kitchen. The ground floor is set up for 14 handicapped accessible SROs and shared baths, a living room/kitchen and an office. The basement has an apartment, offices, and a large room reserved for neighborhood use.

Development Process: The Bowditch School was closed in 1981, one of 27 schools closed in Boston that year. Surrounding property owners were very concerned about the negative impacts of a vacant school on the neighborhood. An activist commu-

nity organization, City Life, was concerned that conversion to market-rate condominiums would gentrify the neighborhood, changing the community character. One view attributed to the city as official policy was that development of market-rate housing was a way for transitional neighborhoods to succeed and prosper. Another view held by City Life activists was that increasing the stock of housing for low- and moderate-income residents was the way for community well-being. These opposing views resonated during a six-year period, which included erec-

The Bowditch School, here, before and after conversion, now provides permanent housing for the homeless in Boston's Jamaica Plain neighborhood.

Sterling/Brown Architects Inc.
Photo: Karosis Photographic

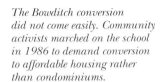

The Bowditch conversion did not come easily. Community activists marched on the school in 1986 to demand conversion to affordable housing rather than condominiums.

Photo: City Life

tion of a tent city, lawsuits, and negotiations by a state legislator. Despite this "tortuous process," as described by one player, what emerged was a converted school of exceptional social utility.

In 1983 the Boston Public Facilities Department designated the school to the private nonprofit Artists Foundation to convert the school to artists' housing and workspace. By 1985 the Artists Foundation proposal fell apart and one of the partners, Michael Robinson of Robinson, Meschan and Sloan, proposed a revised plan. It called for conversion of the school to 27 condominiums, 10 reserved for moderate-income owners. By this time a new mayoral administration was in office and was making provision of low- and moderate-income housing in neighborhoods a major objective. Yet the Public Facilities Department continued with its designation of Robinson as developer and along with his condominium proposal. (PFD maintained it was legally obligated to do so).

Led by City Life and other community activists, strong opposition was voiced at public meetings. In June 1986, a march to the school culminated in a call for erection of a tent city at the Bowditch site to symbolically call for construction of affordable housing for low-income neighborhood residents. The encampment drew as many as a thousand people and lasted one week. That summer the PFD formalized its designation agreement with Robinson and sold Bowditch for $1,000. In fall 1986 the Zoning Board of Appeals granted the developer variances to proceed with the condominium conversion.

At this point, using their rights as abutters (adjoining property owners), City Life and Red Sun Press filed suit to stop the project claiming that the project was unaffordable to the community and the developer's projected profits constituted a giveaway of needed public resources. An injunction obtained at the same time prevented any work on the project pending the outcome of the case.

Following the stock market crash of late 1987, the condo market disappeared in the Boston area and Robinson sought release from the project.

The Public Facilities Department suggested involvement of the Paul Sullivan Trust (PST) as a new developer. The trust is a nonprofit housing developer branch of the Pine Street Inn, a large shelter in Boston. PST develops and manages six buildings in the Boston area as permanent housing for people previously in shelters or transitional housing. The question remained whether or not this potentially volatile proposal would be acceptable to the neighbors. To find out, the PFD enlisted the community's state legislator, Rep. John McDonough, as a mediator/facilitator.

The Negotiation Process: Representative McDonough, a popular elected official with community legitimacy, was known as a supporter of affordable housing programs. His first move was to elicit support from the

Before and after.
Retention of the large window
openings and high ceilings
of the old school provides
abundant light and
spaciousness to the new
apartments and SROs.

Sterling/Brown Architects Inc.
Photo: Karosis Photographic

district's city council member. In December 1987 McDonough called together 15 key people primarily from the Cheshire Street neighborhood association. The Cheshire Street association had supported the condo project and McDonough had in turn supported them through the preceding years of turmoil. So it came as a shock to learn that the condo project was dead and an SRO project was on the table. But because McDonough had been a supporter they listened when he stated: "If you don't want the PST proposal for legitimate reasons, it's not going to go in. Race and income are not legitimate reasons."

The Cheshire Street association was less concerned with the need for condos than with the negative consequences of an abandoned building next door. Yet the prospect of 45 homeless people was threatening to some. McDonough arranged a tour of the Sullivan Trust properties. The competent management and well-maintained projects turned people's attitudes around. By spring 1988 McDonough received word from the Cheshire Street association that it was "open to the idea" of SRO housing. McDonough confidentially informed the other affordable housing

and activist groups who would be involved in the process that talks could proceed on the PST proposal.

By fall 1988, working against a tight deadline, an agreement was reached in private talks to support conversion to an SRO, provided that it would not house persons with mental illness or substance abuse. The proposal was taken before the November meeting of the Neighborhood Council, a locally elected body, for its first public airing.

Although the SRO proposal was generally accepted, the negotiation process was also roundly criticized. Many questions were raised about the proposed operation. PST representatives explained the difference between the careful screening and supervision of SRO residents proposed for the Bowditch and the more lenient entry requirements at the emergency shelter at the Pine Street Inn. Before the December Neighborhood Council meeting, a second tour of Sullivan Trust properties was organized, this time with broader community representation. Just before the December vote, a property owner circulated a petition claiming that the PST proposal was a ploy to build another Pine Street Inn facility. But, in the end, the council voted unanimously to accept the SRO proposal, conditioned on agreement between PST and abutters regarding tenant selection, management, design, and maintenance of the project.

Terms of the Deal: The city sold the property to Robinson, the condominium developer, for $1,000. The eventual SRO manager, Paul Sullivan Trust, purchased the property for $400,000 two years later. A trust comprised of abutters was created to enforce a 30-year restrictive covenant on the property, which bars its use as a shelter. A neighborhood association became the liaison between PST and its neighbors to enforce written agreements on the operation of the project. A meeting room with private entry was made available to the community.

Project development costs totaled $4.4 million. Just over half the amount—$2.3 million—was raised through a syndication of investors gaining advantages through historic rehabilitation and low-income tax credits. The remaining $2.1 million came from state and local funds, including McKinney Act funds, Section 8 funds, and state housing assistance funds. Thirty of the 45 SRO tenants received rent subsidies.

PST relied on its financial advisers, Trinity Financial, to develop a strategy for private equity/public funding. Actual sale of shares in the Bowditch Limited Partnership was handled by Bay State Financial, a subsidiary of The New England Insurance Company. In order to attract investors interested in historic rehabilitation tax credits, PST hired a historic preservation consultant to document Bowditch School's designation in the National Register of Historic Places and consequent qualification for tax act status.

Owner: Bowditch School Limited Partnership

Managers: Paul Sullivan Housing Trust 434 Harrison Avenue Boston, Massachusetts 02118 Mark Baker, Director (617) 574-9004

Before and after of the same foyer location in Bowditch School. Dramatic results can be achieved when faithful attention is given to preserving original wood finishes and lofty ceiling heights.

Sterling/Brown Architects Inc.
Photo: Karosis Photographic

Capitol Hill Senior Resource Center, Denver, Colorado

Current Use: Health and Social Services Center for senior residents of the surrounding community.

Original Use: A three-story brick and stone elementary school named for Ralph Waldo Emerson, built in 1884.

Description: Emerson School's main building is now dedicated to activities and services for senior citizens with offices and a clinic in the basement and first two floors. Portions of these three floors have been extensively remodeled to provide modern space; the remaining area, including the third floor, is scheduled for renovation in 1990. The building is eligible for inclusion in the National Register of Historic Places. The building grounds have been landscaped, a new main entrance has been created with an elevator and handicapped access, and a unique feature of the exterior, Colorado's first sundial, has been restored. Emerson School is located in the Capitol Hill neighborhood, a mature community near downtown Denver with a high proportion of residents over 55 years of age.

The anchor tenant is the Johnson Clinic, which provides medical and dental care for seniors regardless of income. Physician services are provided on a volunteer basis. Dental services are provided through the University of Colorado Dental School. Paid staff include a nurse practitioner and office support. Other tenants include:

■ Medical Care and Research Foundation, the parent organization of the clinic, which develops programs to enhance the quality of life with the least restrictive living arrangements for the elderly.

■ Widowed Persons Service, which provides grief counseling.

■ Parkinson's Disease Association, an education and support group.

■ Colorado Senior Lobby, which reviews state legislation and encourages seniors to lobby.

■ Alcoholics Anonymous.

■ Capitol Hill Community Services, which works with and trains the homeless, feeds people, and prevents financial crises through intervention.

■ Colorado Association of the Blind.

■ Huntington Disease Association.

In addition, the single-story Emerson School annex houses the Capitol Hill Children's Center, a day care and kindergarten serving 60 children, a third of whom are on public assistance of some kind.

Development Process: Emerson School was closed by the Denver public school system in 1970 and left empty until it was sold in 1980. The Denver school system used a sealed bid approach for the sale and received two responsive bids. The first, a bid of $600,000, would have converted the historic school to an adult entertainment center. The second, for $400,000, was a proposal to convert the old school to a health and resource center for the elderly. The school district selected the lower bid made by a new nonprofit organization called Capitol Hill Senior Resources (CHSR), Inc., which had strong community and city health department support. Original board members and leaders included two physicians: Frank McGlone, director of the Medical Care and Research Foundation, and Mildred Doster, a former public school physician.

Capitol Hill Senior Resources made the initial down payment on the property through a no-interest loan from Mildred Doster. CHSR was able to raise approximately $300,000 from a dozen foundations to make initial improvements to the building for its conversion to a senior resource center. Tenants included Senior Resources, the National Stroke Association, and the Johnson Clinic. However, the real estate management of the center proved to be a problem. In 1988 two major tenants moved to larger, more modern locations and a financial crisis threatened the center.

The response was to restructure the board of CHSR, have the Medical Care and Research Foundation pay off outstanding debts, hire a building manager, and raise funds to complete remodeling of the building so that it would serve current and future tenants adequately. The CHSR board was soon chaired by the former mayor of Denver, as well as a bank president and former Denver Broncos general manager. A combination of foundation and block grant funds was obtained to complete the building renovation in 1990.

Terms of the Deal: The school district accepted a $30,000 down payment on the school and agreed to carry a loan for the remaining $370,000 for 16 years at 9 percent annual interest. The loan was paid in full in 1987, nine years early, because of a bequest from one of McGlone's patients. CHSR owns the Emerson School outright, a property valued in excess of $1 million. It is able to rent to nonprofit and volunteer agencies at rents ranging from $3 per square foot to $7.50 per square foot.

Owner: Capitol Hill Senior
Resources, Inc.
1420 Ogden Street
Denver, Colorado 80218
(303) 832-8731

Wallingford Center, Seattle, Washington

Current Use: Mixed-use retail and moderate-income apartments.

Original Use: Three-story wood frame Interlake Elementary School, built in 1905.

Description: A collection of 14 shops are on the first two floors of the old school building, including a bookstore, gift and clothing shops, café and dessert shops, plant store, and restaurants. The school, a Seattle historic landmark listed in the National Register of Historic Places, is sited on a city block facing both commercial and residential streets. The main entrance has been reconfigured to open onto a parking area, while first-floor shops and restaurants spill out onto a pleasant patio and sidewalk level. A public sculpture is installed at the street corner.

The architectural character has been faithfully maintained and restored with attention paid to saving original classroom doors with old brass numbers, the reconstruction of fluted arches on the second floor, and retention of details like brass dust catchers in stairwell corners.

The upper floor has been converted to 24 studio and one-bedroom apartments constructed with Department of Housing and Urban Development Section 312 support to assure moderate-income rent levels.

Development Process: The Interlake School was closed in 1978. The Wallingford Community Council and Wallingford Chamber of Commerce formed a committee to explore reuse options and work with the Seattle Department of Community Development. Their feasibility study suggested retail and housing as appropriate uses. In 1982 the community development department solicited proposals for development of Interlake School through a Request for Proposal process. The RFP explained the kinds of development being sought for the community and

31

Interlake School newly constructed in 1909 in Seattle's Wallingford neighborhood—a gracious building of thick Northwest timbers and all-wood construction.

Photo: Washington State Historical Society

included drawings of potential suitable projects. The proposed Wallingford Center project was selected over a proposal to raze the building and construct a supermarket and another proposal to establish a private school. (School district policy prohibits leases with private schools as this could serve to defeat voluntary desegregation policies.)

Terms of the Deal: The school district sold the school to the developer, Lorig Associates, but leases the land to Lorig for 99 years. The lease terms include an $8,000-per-month payment plus 25 percent of net profit income. The fixed lease payment is adjustable at 10-year intervals based on fair market appraisals.

The $1.6 million project used a combination of private investors and bank loans to finance the project. The existence of 20 percent historic rehabilitation tax credits was a significant factor making the project financially viable. The school district acted essentially as a codeveloper, subordinating its interests to the bank. The city made available Section 312 HUD funds at 5 percent interest to subsidize the apartment units, permitting the project to proceed.

Owners: Lorig Associates
2001 Western Avenue
Seattle, Washington 98101
(206) 728-7660

Seattle Public Schools
Facilities Department
4141 Fourth Avenue South
Seattle, Washington 98134
John Richmond, Manager
(206) 298-7630

The Wallingford Center today: neighborhood shops, moderate-income apartments, attention to architectural detail and historic preservation, and new activity spilling out into the street and into the community.

Photo right: Seattle Times
Photos below: Tonkin/ Koch Architects

When Things Don't Turn Out as Planned

Not every experience in this guidebook deals with successful school conversions. That is because not every school property disposition plan works. It is important to examine failures to seek ways to produce success next time around.

Farragut School Site, San Francisco, California

This 1.4-acre site was viewed by the school district as prime land for market-rate multifamily rental housing. The district's objective was to maximize profit on the land. The cleared site had a market value of approximately $600,000 if the planning commission would permit a density of at least 50 units per acre. However, the mayor suggested that the site would be appropriate for affordable housing. The planning commission approved a density of 42 units per acre with the condition that child care facilities, covered parking, and an auditorium be provided.

The district had difficulty finding a developer to purchase the site with the restrictions imposed by the city. The district finally sold the land for $125,000, about one-fifth of what it had hoped to get. After the sale had closed, the affordable housing groups found the economics of the city-imposed conditions did not work and lobbied the mayor and commission to change its conditions. The zoning was eventually changed to permit a density of 48 units per acre. The covered parking, child care, and auditorium conditions were deleted. Since the net effect of the experience was to lower the cost of housing on the site by reducing the land price, a cynical analysis might conclude that the city had achieved its objective of low-cost housing by intentionally forcing the school district to subsidize the project. However, it is just as likely that the city really did want all the public benefits originally required on the site. Nevertheless, ill will and mistrust developed between the city and the school district.

As we have seen in the successful Palo Alto example, a city can compensate the school district for not developing its property to maximize value. In Arlington, Virginia, the county worked to find the right property and additional funding to conduct a land trade. And in Palo Alto and Seattle, formal mechanisms at the elected official and staff level permitted resolution of Farragut-type conflicts before they happened.

Owner: San Francisco Unified School District
Property Management Department
801 Toland Street
San Francisco, California 94124
Lawrence Jacobsen, Manager
(415) 695-2356

Ravenswood High School, East Palo Alto, California

Ravenswood High School was closed in 1976 by the Sequoia Union High School District, which operates high schools in several incorporated communities as well as in San Mateo County. School-age population in the six high schools in the district had declined from around 12,000 to 6,000, and two schools were closed. Ravenswood was geographically most distant from the center of the district. It also was situated in an unincorporated community of about 20,000 people just east of Palo Alto, which although adjacent to this well-off city, was about as different an area as could be imagined. East Palo Alto was considered a ghetto; more than 80 percent black, it is one of the poorest sections of the San Jose-San Francisco peninsula area.

The 30-acre Ravenswood site was leased to groups including a day care facility, a senior center, and a printing operation during the period 1976–84. The site was also vandalized. By 1984 the district decided to sell the site for $3.6 million dollars for a light industry and recreation development that would take advantage of the property's location adjacent to the Bayshore Freeway. The school district saw an opportunity to generate revenue from unused property. East Palo Alto saw differently.

East Palo Alto incorporated as a city in 1983. One of its first official acts was to downzone the Ravenswood property to recreation and open space, thereby scuttling the school district's sale plans. The new city wanted to gain control of the site. By zoning for open space the city could take advantage of the Naylor Act, a California law that allows public entities to purchase up to 30 percent of surplused school sites for open space and recreation use for only 25 percent of the value of the property. The school district promptly sued the city for inverse condemnation.

East Palo Alto applied for and received $1 million of county-administered community development block grant funds to consummate the purchase of the school. At the same time, the validity of the elections incorporating the city was challenged in court, threatening the existence of the city just as it was signing a major real estate transaction. At this critical point, the city, county, and school district entered into a creative agreement.

In the 1985 agreement, the three parties divided the property into three parts and settled on a purchase price of $1.83 million. Ten-acre Parcel A would consist of the school buildings and be zoned institutional. Eleven-acre Parcel B would be zoned open space. Eight-acre Parcel C would be zoned low- and moderate-income multifamily housing. The school district would prepare all needed background reports for the rezone request. The city would ex-

pedite the rezoning and pay the district $1 million (of block grant funds) for the open space and housing land. Upon receipt of this payment and the execution of a development agreement for Parcel C, the district would turn over title of the school buildings as well. The city would then make payments of approximately $200,000 annually to the district for four years. The county would take over the city's obligations should the city cease to exist during the term of the agreement.

By 1990 the city of East Palo Alto made its final payment. However, the $231,000 final payment was placed in escrow pending a development agreement for Parcel C in accordance with new plans to redevelop the site into mixed-use commercial and residential uses. The city solicited developer interest through an RFP, and several developers responded. The city would form a partnership with the developer who would bear the pre-development costs. The city wished to meet a variety of objectives including creating jobs, increasing the tax base, upgrading the housing stock, and improving recreational opportunities.

The district's school board still sought greater compensation from the city through its pending court case. The city's settlement offer of more than $1 million was rejected. As of summer 1990, the school remained mostly vacant with school offices and a senior center filling some space; the property was undeveloped, and further settlement conferences were scheduled.

Contacts: Linda Hamilton-Rahi
Deputy City Manager
City of East Palo Alto
2415 University Avenue
East Palo Alto, California 94303
(415) 853-3100

Sherrill Houghton
Assistant Superintendent,
Administrative Services
Sequoia Union High School District
480 James Avenue
Redwood City, California 94062
(415) 369-1411, Extension 217

Scottsdale High School, Scottsdale, Arizona

Scottsdale High School, closed in 1983, sits in the middle of one of the nation's most prosperous cities. The school district carefully prepared a strategy for managing this prime asset believing that with this 38-acre site it possessed "location, location, location." District officials did everything right. They worked closely with the city of Scottsdale coordinating the site with a new downtown plan and zoning. They hired expert consultants to assess retail, hotel, office, and commercial market feasibility. They retained a consultant to act as manager of the RFP process. They prepared a four-color glossy request-for-development prospectus in which they spelled out their desire for a mixed-use development based on a ground lease that would provide long-term revenue to the district. They provided site location, zoning, financial, and marketing data to prospective developers. They circulated the RFP nationally in 1987. Nevertheless, in 1990 the site remained vacant.

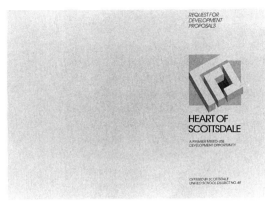

Few school owners have been more thorough in marketing their properties than Scottsdale, Arizona, Public Schools. This prospectus includes an artist's conception of future site development.

What went wrong? Probably the single most significant factor was a downturn in the Phoenix-area economy in the late 1980s, which forced developers to assess risks more cautiously. In response to the RFP, the district negotiated with the national real estate developer, Trammell Crow, on terms for a mixed-use development lease. The developer proposed nominal lease payments over the first few years gradually increasing as the start-up and high-risk period of the new development ended. The school district felt it needed larger amounts of money sooner as it was "strapped for cash." At the same time the city was enforcing its strict development controls for the downtown area. After months of negotiations, the developer walked away from the negotiations. Had the local economy remained strong, it is likely that negotiations would have succeeded. But a second issue arose from the district's point of view and that was the sense of vulnerability negotiating with a giant developer, the sense that "they [the developers] are always going to come out ahead."

In 1989 the district went to the voters asking authorization to sell the property. Recognizing the difficulties in negotiating a lease arrangement, the voters approved the sale (several years earlier voters had permitted the district only to lease). In 1990 the district will offer the 38 acres for sale as an entire site. If the district is unable to get the price they seek for the whole site, it will offer smaller parcels for sale over time. The dis-

trict retained real estate economists to estimate the value of the land in 1990 and the value which would accrue to the district if it acted as developer and sold pieces of the site over the next 10 years. This information provides a benchmark in the sale negotiations that lie ahead.

Upon successful sale, funds will be invested in a restricted fund by the county treasurer, a percentage of which is available for district use each year.

Contact: Robert C. Hubley
Assistant Superintendent of
Business Services
Scottsdale Public Schools
P.O. Box 15428
Phoenix, Arizona 85060
(602) 952-6144

Gary Roe, Planning Director
City of Scottsdale
7447 East Indian School Road
Scottsdale, Arizona 85251
(602) 994-7831

Albuquerque High School, Albuquerque, New Mexico

As Albuquerque's only public high school from 1914 until 1948, this five-building complex sits deteriorating on seven acres in the heart of downtown. The buildings, which are all listed in the National Register of Historic Places, were closed by the Albuquerque Public Schools in 1976 and traded to a local developer for property near another high school. The site represented a prime development opportunity. In the early 1980s it was slated to be converted to Harrington Square, consisting of offices and small shops, but this proved unsuccessful. In 1984 two local developers, Sproul and Brown, joined forces with a Boston investor, Charles Hill, to develop Banner Square. With a development budget of $19.9 million, this project was to have been the state's largest rehabilitation project with an impressive mix of restaurants, boutiques, a movie theater, health club, and offices. Its financing featured $10 million in city-backed metropolitan redevelopment bonds plus historic rehabilitation tax credits. However this proposal also did not materialize.

As the buildings continued to decay, Albuquerque's real estate market slumped, and the city government became actively involved. "It's been sitting there for years, deteriorating at a rapid rate," said a member of the city's development team. "If anything is going to be done, it really falls on the city now. The fear is, if the city doesn't get involved, the private sector won't make it happen, and we may lose the buildings." The city be-

gan negotiating with the owner for purchase at a price somewhere between $2 and $3 million.

In fall 1989, the city council created a citizens' task force to examine the reuse potential of the school site and make a recommendation as to the feasibility of city ownership. The task force report was to have been presented to the council sometime in summer 1990.

In the 1990 state legislative session, $345,000 was appropriated for reuse-purchase of the buildings. However, as of June 1990, the city had yet to enter into a purchase agreement with the owner.

Concurrently, a private developer was discussing the possibility of buying the property, rehabilitating the space for government offices, and

In the heart of downtown, Albuquerque High School awaits transformation.

Photo: City of Albuquerque

entering into a lease arrangement with city and county governments. As part of the agreement, the leasing cost would be fixed for 20 years; at the end of that time, the property would be returned to the city. A proposal such as this had to be voted on by the public, and it was unclear if this could occur within the developer's time frame.

One of the major difficulties in redevelopment of the buildings in New Mexico is the state's anti-donation clause, which prohibits governmental bodies from directly or indirectly benefiting the private sector.

Contact: Victoria Prinz, Planner
Redevelopment and Planning
Department
City of Albuquerque
P.O. Box 1293
Albuquerque, New Mexico 87103
(505) 768-3283

The city of Albuquerque wants to buy the seven-acre campus of the Albuquerque High School. The school was closed in 1976 and has been the subject of a variety of private redevelopment plans.

Photo: City of Albuquerque

Valuable Properties

When examining facilities portfolios, school districts often find they possess properties in valuable locations. These school sites may be in downtown locations or along the path of postwar growth. They may be of historical or commercial value. While not every district has such properties, they can offer huge income potential, and their financial negotiation is frequently held to close scrutiny by all parties. In two of the instances described here, the yield is more than $1 million dollars in annual lease payments to school districts. While such circumstances may be attributed to plain luck, it may also be possible to anticipate increasing commercial value of certain properties as part of an asset management plan. At the same time these situations offer ways for cities to revitalize downtown cores while supporting school district operations.

BIG-CITY DOWNTOWN CORE

San Francisco Centre/Fifth and Market, San Francisco, California

Current Use: Downtown shopping complex.

Original Use: School facility, closed in 1906.

Description: The San Francisco School District owns the 76,000-square-foot site at the corner of Fifth and Market in downtown San Francisco. The location lies just at the edge of the thriving retail core yet had been plagued by panhandlers and alcoholics. The site, long envisioned by downtown boosters and city planners as a key to a retailing renaissance, is now occupied by a 10-level, 670,000-square-foot, $140 million shopping center known as San Francisco Centre, which opened in 1988. The anchor tenant, Nordstrom, occupies half the space, with additional space for about 90 restaurants and shops.

Development Process: A major Los Angeles–based shopping center developer, Sheldon Gordon, expressed interest in the Fifth and Market site in the late 1970s in meetings with the mayor and city officials. The school district created a blue-ribbon panel to recommend a list of qualified and interested developers for the site. The panel included representatives of major downtown properties, financial institutions, the city, and

The San Francisco School District receives $1 million yearly for the lease of its downtown site at 5th and Market. The Nordstrom store and about 90 other shops opened here in 1988.

Photo: David Carlson

regional entities, including the Port of Oakland and the Golden Gate Bridge and Transportation Authority and the school district's consulting real estate economist. Having such a panel was important to the district as it legitimized its actions and rendered important technical and policy advice dealing in a high risk, high profile, and high dollar arena. Gordon's prior interest in the site had the effect of limiting other proposals, and the panel recommended negotiations with the Gordon firm to determine terms of a lease.

Terms of the Deal: The basic annual lease payment is $1 million for 75 years (50 years plus options for 15 and 10 years). Escalation is tied to the Consumer Price Index or a percentage of rental income. The developer has the right to sell the lease with the school district's approval.

Owner: San Francisco Unified School District
Property Management Department
801 Toland Street
San Francisco, California 94124
Lawrence Jacobsen, Manager
(415) 695-2356

COMMERCIAL STRIP DEVELOPMENT

Oak Tree Village, Seattle, Washington

Current Use: Community shopping center.

Original Use: Oak Lake Elementary School, built in 1914 and 1927 with additions in the 1930s and 1940s.

Description: The original school structure was removed and replaced by a variety of shops, a cinema complex, and a supermarket on the eight-acre

Developer Selection

Some states require school districts to accept the high bidder for property sale or lease. For most school districts and municipalities, it is preferable to be able to negotiate the sale or lease with the most responsive, preferred developer. Districts often find it important to obtain the professional services of real estate economists, appraisers, financial analysts, and real estate attorneys in the developer selection and negotiation process.

One property manager who has been saddled with highest bidder requirements in sophisticated urban real estate transactions concludes that the "deal should go to the second highest bidder because he knows when to stop!" The inexperienced developer may overbid to obtain the lease only to see the project fall apart because of an inability to make the finances

site. The 24-hour grocery store, with its espresso bar, café, and floral shop, was voted "Best Supermarket in Seattle" and has had a major positive impact on the area north of downtown along Highway 99.

Development Process: The Oak Lake School was closed in 1982 and categorized for disposition because of its deteriorated physical condition and its desirable commercial location. In 1983 a Request for Proposal was circulated offering the site for long-term lease or sale. Three possible development options were suggested:

work. In such cases the district, developer, and community lose out.

The Ground Lease

The option of leasing land has great appeal to some developers and little appeal to others. Finding the right match and providing necessary freedom in the lease agreement are keys to making ground leases work. One shopping mall developer looks for inexpensive land to control over the long term and does not like ground leases. Smaller or specialty developers may not want land ownership and may welcome a lease arrangement that permits them smaller payments during the first few years followed by gradually increasing annual payments as cash flow from the project improves. Another important consideration for both parties is whether and under what conditions the lease can be sold and profits realized from the increased value of the land.

■ mixed-use auto oriented, commercial and office use;

■ warehousing and light manufacturing park; or

■ mixed-use commercial and residential.

In 1984 the school district selected a proposal from the Rainier Fund to build a shopping center on the site and entered into an option agreement to permit the developer to obtain needed zoning changes. Rezoning was approved by the city and a lease agreement signed.

Special Needs Housing in a Wealthy Neighborhood

In 1989 the Boston school system surplused its first schools in eight years. One of these is Faneuil School on Beacon Hill. Beacon Hill is a very fashionable historic district where a parking condo (ownership of a single parking stall) recently sold for $189,000. One development option under consideration is to request proposals for development of a mixed-housing complex. The historic school building would be converted to 27 market-rate condominiums. New construction on the site would include a below-ground parking garage with 32 new single-room

occupancy (SRO) units above the garage. A portion of the SRO housing would be reserved for people with Acquired Immune Deficiency Syndrome (AIDS). The idea of building a lodging house (SRO hotel) on Beacon Hill has historical precedence since such facilities used to be located in this district.

A feasibility analysis of such an option was prepared by the Public Facilities Department for internal review. Will it emerge from consideration to the RFP or public meeting process? To find out more, contact Kathy Calhoun, Public Facilities Department, 15 Beacon Street, Seventh Floor, Boston, Massachusetts 02108.

Terms of the Deal: The ground lease for the site is for 50 years. It calls for the district to receive $120,000 in annual payments adjusted at 10-year intervals. Additionally, the district receives income related to the success of the project as would a co-developer. A percentage (between 15 and 50 percent is the range in the Seattle School District's lease agreements) of net earnings above the annual payment is made to the district. The project was privately financed by the developer.

Owner: Seattle Public Schools Facilities Department
4141 Fourth Avenue South
Seattle, Washington 98134
John Richmond, Manager
(206) 298-7630

ENGINEERING CAMPUS
IN A SMALL CITY

Westinghouse Engineering Center, Sunnyvale, California

Current Use: Engineer and support offices for Westinghouse Marine Division.

Original Use: Sunnyvale High School built in 1956.

Description: The old Sunnyvale High School campus is made up of one-story classroom buildings connected by covered walkways and open courtyards. It includes a theater used by Westinghouse for large meetings and rented to the community as well. It also includes a gymnasium building, three swimming pools, locker facilities, tennis courts, and athletic fields. The site totals 40 acres.

Development Process: The school was closed in 1980 by the Fremont Union High School District, which serves six municipalities in the Santa Clara-Silicon Valley area. Sunnyvale High School sat vacant for one year; vandalism occurred, gangs hung out, and community support grew for an alternative use. Westinghouse Marine Division, which had a large manufacturing facility a few miles from the school site, was looking for a new facility for its engineering division composed of 800 engineers and 24-hour security control.

In its search for space Westinghouse investigated the closed school. The site offered several advantages including proximity to its main plant, sufficient size, ease of security, sufficient parking, square-foot costs approximately 20 percent below the prevailing market, and the amenities of athletic facilities and open space.

The factor that closed the deal was the willingness of the school district to assume the role of real estate developer and make the tenant improvements that Westinghouse required. An additional factor in the successful negotiation of a lease was strong support for the new use among neighbors and city government. Westinghouse held two public meetings to explain its plans; the combination of community employment and an end of vandalism to the site were viewed favorably by the community. The city of Sunnyvale granted the school district a use permit and renovation proceeded.

In 1981 the school district gutted the buildings, removed classroom walls, put in carpet, dropped ceilings, and installed new air-conditioning systems to meet Westinghouse design specifications. A new two-story 14,000-square-foot building was constructed at a cost of $1.5 million. The campus, which once housed between 1,500 and 2,000 students, was secured with fencing and cameras and was now ready for its new resident population of 800 engineers and support staff.

Terms of the Deal: The parties hold a 10-year master lease with an option for two-year extensions. The lease payments net the school district $2 million annually after the following expenses are deducted:

■ $200,000 — maintenance of air conditioning, plumbing, and pools;

■ $65,000 — possessory interest tax to state of California (owed because the district earns revenue from the lease); and

■ $22,000 — penalty to the state for not using the site as a school.

Westinghouse is responsible for internal landscaping in courtyards and similar areas, electrical maintenance, janitors, some plumbing, and maintenance of lockers, gymnasium, and other recreational facilities.

An unforeseen problem has developed surrounding liability for the use of the athletic facilities resulting in closure of the pools for the employees and the athletic fields and track to the community. Westinghouse allowed community use of the athletic fields until they were sued by individuals who sustained injuries on the fields. The company contracted with the local YMCA to operate the

pools for its employees. A suit was filed claiming that an excessive amount of chlorine gas was used in the pools. Westinghouse responded by closing the pools.

In Silicon Valley it is not uncommon for employers to offer recreational activities as part of the work environment. Firms providing this amenity support this function with staff committed to organizing and supervising these activities. Westinghouse assumed a facility capable of providing "country club" amenities but was not organizationally structured to manage it. Public access to the athletic fields is a subject under discussion between the district and the city preparatory to lease renegotiation in 1992. The city owns a 13-acre park adjacent to the athletic fields, but was reluctant to take on additional responsibilities when the original Westinghouse lease was made. Now with new community pressure for public access, the nearly 22 acres of athletic fields could be brought under the jurisdiction of the Sunnyvale parks and recreation department, thus relieving Westinghouse of liability concerns and providing public access.

Owner: Fremont Union High
School District
589 Fremont
Sunnyvale, California 94087
Mike Raffetto, Assistant Superintendent for Business
(408) 522-2210

Lessee: Westinghouse Marine Division
Engineering Center
401 East Hendy Avenue
P.O. Box 3499
Sunnyvale, California 94088
Frank Rodrigues, Facilities Manager
(408) 735-2608

Sumner and Magruder Schools, Washington, D.C.

Current Use: New office building and historic museum.

Original Use: Sumner Elementary and Secondary School and Magruder Elementary School.

Description: The Sumner and Magruder schools are located opposite the National Geographic Building on the corner of 17th and M streets in downtown Washington, D.C., on land estimated in 1989 to be worth over $300 a square foot. Both school buildings are over 100 years old and are listed in the National Register of Historic Places. Sumner School was built in 1871 and was named for U.S. Sen. Charles Sumner, abolitionist and advocate for integration and nondiscrimination. Sumner School remains the best existing and least altered example of a school in the nation's capital built after the Civil War for the public education of children of former slaves. It has housed an elementary school, a preparatory and secondary school where the first high school graduation for black students was held, a four-year teachers' college, and the headquarters for the superintendent and the Board of Trustees of Colored Schools of Washington and Georgetown. Its Great Hall auditorium on the third floor was used for community meetings and lectures.

Today the Sumner School stands fully restored as the Washington, D. C., public schools' official museum and archives. The neighboring Magruder School, built in 1887 of similar 19th-century brick, now serves as the street facade and entrance to the new office building complex, which wraps around and in back of the two schools. This complex provides the economic stimulus that made this adaptive use possible. Magruder was discontinued as a classroom building in 1953 and closed in 1980.

The mirror glass-curtain wall of the nine-story office building is set back 90 feet from M Street, forming a backdrop for the Magruder building. "It's an attempt to make a big building as invisible as possible," explained Warren Cox, partner in the architectural firm Hartman/Cox, which won awards for the design.

Development Process: In June 1978 a private school occupying Sumner School moved out leaving the building vacant. In 1979 the school was placed in the National Register of Historic Places. This proved to be an important step, because that summer part of the roof collapsed, and the city notified the school board that the building was "imminently dangerous and unsafe and should be razed" within 24 hours. The school board went to court and received a restraining order, based on the structure's historical significance, to prevent demolition.

In Washington, D.C., the school board is responsible for maintaining school buildings and grounds, but the city's Department of General Services (DGS) is responsible for the disposition of all school buildings. By 1980 school board and DGS officials began meeting to hammer out a way to save the school with such histori-

Condemned to the wrecking ball in 1979, Sumner School, built in 1871 to educate children of former slaves, stands fully restored as a public meeting place and historic museum.

Sumner School and its younger sister Magruder School [opposite], both in the National Register of Historic Places, are integrated into a private, prestigious office complex in the heart of the Washington, D.C., business district.

Photos/top and right: Warren Jaeger Photography Inc.

cal significance in a predominantly black city. After a year of negotiation, the two departments signed a memorandum of understanding stating that if the board relinquished control of Sumner School, DGS would not sell it. Further, a review panel was established comprising two members from the board of education and two from the city government; the panel would have the responsibility for soliciting and reviewing development proposals for the Sumner-Magruder site.

In 1981 a Request for Proposals was released, a joint product of the school board and DGS. The review panel selected five finalists and recommended a joint-venture development proposal from Hartman/Cox Architects, Boston Properties Developer, First City Properties, and Met-

ropolitan African Methodist Episcopal Church. The development team included a minority law firm and the church that originally had owned the land on which the Sumner School was built. The church, now located a block from the site, gained Sunday parking for church services and a reduction of its debt from new building construction under the partnership agreement. The partnership gained support of one of the largest black congregations.

Negotiations to craft a ground lease agreement continued for 15 months, a function of the complexity of the development project and the care with which the parties approached this "first time" venture. The school board and city government agreed to support the developer's request for a rezone of the one-acre site, which took another year. Construction began in 1984 and was completed in 1985.

Terms of the Deal: The one-acre site is leased to the developer for 80 years at a yearly rent of $1.3 million. This ground rent is forgiven by the district until the costs of renovation of Sumner School and accrued operating and financing expenses are reached. The public benefit received for the estimated first 25 years of the lease agreement is the fully renovated and restored Sumner Museum facility. Project construction of the school cost $7.5 million; annual operating costs are approximately $400,000. The office complex is fully occupied.

Owner: District of Columbia Schools, Sumner School Museum and Archives
17th & M Streets NW
Washington, D.C. 20036
Richard Hurlbut, Director
(202) 727-3419

Lessee: Boston Properties
500 E Street S.W., No. 850
Washington, D.C. 20024
Robert Burke, Senior Vice President
(202) 646-7600

Small Towns

A closed school in a small town can have dramatic impacts. The resources to save or redevelop the building are often difficult to find. In small rural locations consolidation of schools into more modern districts confirms the fate of many communities as relics of a bygone era. For some small communities every effort is made to catch up with new technologies that represent future economic growth and well being. For others, it is a battle to retain the small-town way of life threatened by metropolitan growth and the rapidity of change. In the cases that follow, three small towns are highlighted: two have less than 400 residents, the third has around 10,000.

Dunn, North Carolina (pop. 10,000), is located in central North Carolina and supported economic development by turning an old school into a business incubator center.

Port Costa, California (pop. 250), is located at the northeast edge of the San Francisco metropolitan area and is battling to protect itself from unwanted growth and suburbia.

Gully, Minnesota (pop. 150), is located in north central Minnesota and revitalized its main street by converting the closed school into a

home for the grocery store, café, and post office, and eight units of senior citizen housing.

One common theme for each town has been support from one or more state agencies, because financial resources for the project simply did not exist within the municipality.

BUSINESS INCUBATOR IN A SMALL TOWN

Triangle South Small Business Enterprise Center, Dunn, North Carolina

Current Use: Small business incubator.

Original Use: Magnolia Avenue Elementary School, built in 1918.

Description: The two-story brick and stone elementary school housed kindergarten through third grades in its 18 classrooms for nearly 70 years until it was closed in 1984. Three other elementary schools serve Dunn, a small (All-America City awardee) town of 10,000 located southeast of Raleigh, North Carolina. The converted school offers 18,500 square feet of refurbished office, manufacturing, and meeting space to start-up businesses at below-market lease arrangements. New businesses benefit from shared support services such as copying, secretarial, and phone services, and a central location for a period of up to three years, at which point the business should be able to emerge into the general business community. In order to nurture the young businesses, management and training services have been made available through Central Carolina Community College's Small Business Center and the Small Business Technology Development Center at

Fayetteville State University. Business tenants have included Central Carolina Catering, Professional Hearing Aid Center, Information Systems International, Aquaglide Sport Ski Ltd., a private investigator, Academics Plus Learning Center, a financial planner, and a construction firm.

Development Process: The story of the Triangle South Enterprise Center revolves around state and local efforts to encourage economic development and school and county officials who cooperated to make the project happen. The Dunn Area Committee of 100 was catalyst for the incubator center and manages it today. The Committee of 100 is a nonprofit organization comprised of private business leaders and public officials concerned about economic development in Harnett County. They sought to take advantage of new state legislation that encourages assistance to rural areas through funding and technical assistance for incubator business centers. Eight such centers exist statewide. The legislation created the Technological Development Authority (TDA) in the state's Department of Commerce. TDA can fund incubator centers up to $200,000, providing they are run by a nonprofit entity in a publicly owned facility. The Committee of 100 requested that the school district transfer title of the Magnolia Avenue School to Harnett County, and both entities agreed. The Community College Small Business Center became involved in the project as well. Development of the center was started, and rehabilitation began in 1987.

Terms of the Deal: The State TDA provided a $200,000 capital improvements grant. The appraised value of the school property was used as the match. A second-year grant of $50,000 came from state legislature discretionary funds. The staff director and secretary were paid through the community college. Harnett County agreed to lease the building to the Committee of 100 for five years at $1 per year. Cost of dividing classrooms into professional offices was approximately $3,000 per classroom. Rents are between $4.50 and $5 per square foot annually, comparable to prevailing rents in the Dunn area; however, incubator rents include office support services and financial and business counseling.

Manager: Triangle South Enterprise Center
600 South Magnolia Avenue
Dunn, North Carolina 28334
Nancy Blackman, Executive Director
(919) 892-8775

Port Costa Elementary School [below], built in 1911, faces the small-town public square Plaza del Hambre. The column capital [left] is a powerful reminder of the elaborate decorative motifs that make old buildings so appealing.

Photo: Lewis Stewart

HISTORIC SCHOOL
IN A VERY SMALL TOWN

Port Costa Elementary School, Port Costa, California

Current Use: Center for town meetings and voting.

Original Use: Port Costa Elementary School.

Description: The two-story wood frame, brick- and stucco-faced, 15,000-square-foot schoolhouse was built in 1911, housing kindergarten through eighth grades until its closure in 1966. Port Costa is a town of 250 residents located at the northeastern edge of the San Francisco Bay Area in rapidly growing Contra

Costa County. The town's 80 registered voters were unable to stop the creation of a unified school district in 1965. One of the district's first steps was to consolidate school operations and close Port Costa's only

school. Today the 19 school-age children in town are bused to schools in neighboring Rodeo or Crockett. The school sits on 2.2 acres of land and includes a playground with large swings to form the town's public

45

square, Plaza del Hambre. The recreation room, kitchen, and a bathroom in the building are available for community use, recreational purposes, and as the location of a voting precinct. The remaining space is currently mothballed awaiting fundraising and rehabilitation efforts by the Port Costa Conservation Society, its new owners.

Port Costa Elementary School, slightly overgrown on the outside [below]; a classically proportioned sitting room awaits the visitor inside [left].

Photo: Lewis Stewart

Development Process: The John Swett Unified School District had no further use for the old Port Costa school after 1966. Old desks, files, and other items were stored there, and the school was used as a community meeting place, Halloween "haunted house," and polling place. But the fact that the district had surplus space among its assets made it impossible for it to receive state funds for school construction. The district wanted to unload the property. The Port Costa Conservation Society, the 100-member nonprofit organization dedicated to preserving the town's character and surrounding environment, wanted to protect the school and use it as an interpretive center. But how could it afford the $2.2 million the school was valued at in 1986?

The answer lay in a creative solution devised by the district, the society, and the local state assemblyman who obtained passage of a new law as part of the California Education Code.

Prior to the new law, the school district had to sell its property at fair market value. Under the new law passed in 1986, the district can sell an old school for its original develop-

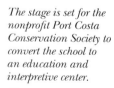

The stage is set for the nonprofit Port Costa Conservation Society to convert the school to an education and interpretive center.

Photo: Lewis Stewart

Since 1966, when the unified school district closed the Port Costa Elementary School, it has been used as a community meeting place, Halloween "haunted house," and polling place. A new California law permits nonprofit organizations to purchase and manage surplus schools for the original development costs—in this case $13,250.

Photo: Lewis Stewart

ment cost if it has historical significance and a local nonprofit community organization will maintain it.

Applying the same energy to historical research as to saving unspoiled open space around their town, conservation society volunteers found that the school's architect, William Wilde, had designed other San Francisco Bay Area schools and that the building had historical significance. A nomination was made and the school was listed in the National Register of Historic Places in 1988.

The volunteers learned more. The original land for the school cost $750 in 1886 and the construction cost an-

other $12,500 in 1911; and a portion of the property was dedicated for public use as part of Plaza El Hambre. Now the society knew it had to raise $13,250 to purchase the old school. This it did with a quilt raffle, barbecue, square dance, and fund-raising letter campaign. Preparation of the historic designation form was supported in part by a grant from the National Trust for Historic Preservation, and a local foundation donated a sizable gift toward saving the school.

Terms of the Deal: The Port Costa Conservation Society paid the school district $13,250, for which it received title to the school and the responsibility to maintain the building for at least 25 years or lose the building. The John Swett Unified School District gave the state of California $13,250 and received in return $1 million for renovations to its high school. The society now had to embark on a campaign to raise about $500,000 to renovate the building and develop the desired community and environmental interpretive center. Annual operation and maintenance costs to keep the school partially open ran about $3,000 until the 1989 earthquake, when insurance rate increases pushed the annual budget to $10,000. Annual operating funds are raised through barbecues, square dances, and other events. The newest effort is selling some of the chairs, desks, and other artifacts from 89 years of school history.

Owner: Port Costa
Conservation Society
P.O. Box 36
Port Costa, California 94569
Mary Powell, Development Officer
(415) 787-2880

MIXED-USE FACILITY IN A SMALL TOWN

Gully Center, Gully, Minnesota

Current Use: Elderly housing and stores.

Original Use: Gully Public Elementary School, built in 1915 with addition in 1965.

Description: The original school is a small, 1,620-square-foot, wood frame structure with a gabled roof, which was enlarged in 1965 with a 12,800-square-foot, one-story masonry addition. The school was closed in the early 1980s. The 3,700-square-foot gymnasium was converted to the town's grocery store and café. The classrooms are now eight affordable apartments for senior citizens as well as the town's only post office.

Development Process: Gully is a town of less than 200 people struggling to survive in one of the state's poorest areas. Events between 1980 and 1983 seemed designed as some kind of cosmic test to see if this little community could survive. The closure of its only school was followed in quick succession by threatened condemnation of the local post office facilities, a fire that destroyed the town's only grocery store, and the near bankruptcy of the town's only café. Times were bleak indeed.

But the local citizenry rose to the occasion with the assistance of the region's community action program, the Inter-County Community Council, Inc., and a local contractor-turned-developer. The plan was to redevelop the town by turning the closed school into a retail center with low- and moderate-income housing

for elderly renters. The $380,000 redevelopment project was conceived as a public-private partnership involving the city, county, and state, and local businesses. The city agreed to issue tax increment financing bonds to purchase the building from the private owners and in turn sell it to the local developer. Sale of the building served the goal of state-authorized tax increment financing to spur private development, and it also recognized the limits of a very small town to negotiate and administer a lease agreement.

The state's Small Cities Fund (state block grant funds) provided renovation funds that were combined with Rental Rehabilitation Program money and the developer's private investment. Relocation costs were born by the post office, the grocery store owner, and, in the case of the café, by the city of Gully, which actually operated and moved the business in order to save the town's informal meeting place. HUD Section 8 rental rehabilitation funds were applied to the apartment renovation, and rental certificates were available to the tenants. (HUD Section 8 pro-

grams offered a range of subsidies to provide rental housing for moderate income people.)

Terms of the Deal: The city purchased the building for $45,000 from private owners and deeded it to the developer, Gully Center Inc., for less than $1,000. Relocation and leasehold improvements totaling $115,000 were borne by the post office and grocery store and by the city on behalf of the café, which has since become a major success. Construction and renovation to the building totaled around $200,000, of which $60,000 was the developer's private investment and the remainder was state and county block grant funds. The Inter-County Community Council assisted the city in managing and administering the project, which is now privately operated.

Contact: Leona Humphrey
Department of Trade and Economic Development
900 American Center Building
150 East Kellogg Boulevard
St. Paul, Minnesota 55101
(612) 296-5005

An old school stage transformed into a residents' lounge.

Sterling /Brown Architects Inc.
Photo: Karosis Photographic

Anticipating Change

If there is a central theme to this guide, it is that communities change and that creative use can be made of important focal points such as school buildings. But must conversion to new community uses—housing, retail, or social service space—happen on a crisis basis? Can school buildings be designed to serve multiple purposes during the course of their expected lives? Although almost every community in the country has experienced a school closure, new school buildings continue to be constructed as single-function facilities with little thought to future conversion.

It is possible to anticipate change by designing school buildings for multiple uses over time. Two school districts that have done this are Dublin, Ohio, and Arvada, Colorado. They are featured here as models for planning for changing community needs.

FUTURE OFFICES

Dublin, Ohio

Dublin is a rapidly growing suburb of Columbus that has tripled in size from 15,000 to 45,000 people during the period 1980 to 1990. The Dublin School District has built five elementary and two middle schools, and one high school and is planning to build an additional three elementary, two middle, and two high schools by the year 2000. Recognizing that the school-age population will peak and then decline after the turn of the century, the school board adopted a policy of advocating school designs that could fit easily into the surrounding residential areas and also be converted to such uses as health care facilities, small business offices, child care centers, and community centers.

The Dublin schools' master plan emphasizes joint investment in property between the city and the school district. In two cases, city parks are constructed adjacent to school buildings. The district's office of operations and development works with the city's planning and zoning department to zone school sites with potential dual zoning at the time of construction so that future uses are permissible. The district and city are jointly planning and funding a 34-acre vehicle maintenance yard for school buses and city vehicles. "It's not as easy as doing it on your own . . . but for the taxpayers and the long term it's better," said Joe Riedel, the district's assistant superintendent.

One new school, Scottish Corners, is designed to look like an integral part of the residential subdivision surrounding it, complete with dormer windows and skylighted turrets. The building's steel frame has few interior load-bearing walls; "de-mountable" partitions separating classrooms make future reconfiguration and "complete remodeling" an easy option. Community use of the school is also enhanced by design: the activities wing of the school adjacent to the public park can be used as a community center on evenings and weekends with a movable partition securing other parts of the school space.

COTTAGE SCHOOLS

Arvada, Colorado

Adjacent to Denver, Arvada has a population in excess of 100,000. Today, 16 subsidized houses, once "cottage schools," provide homes for large families in residential communities. In 1950, 39 school districts northwest of Denver were consolidated into the Jefferson County School District. At that time Arvada had a population of 2,360, but the county was growing and the district began an ambitious program of school construction. Concerned that as residential communities matured new schools would be under-enrolled, the district built new schools designed for a lower capacity than the estimated peak enrollment in their attendance area.

Then the district, local municipalities, and developers agreed to implement a "cottage school" concept, whereby satellite primary units for elementary schools were constructed in new residential developments. Standard frame construction similar to that used in a single-family home was utilized. Each cottage contained two classrooms and a basement; brick veneer blended the building into its surroundings. Typically, two to four such cottages were clustered in one location with play areas located in the "back yards." As the residential areas matured, these cottage schools were intended to become residences.

In total, Jefferson School District constructed 88 cottage schools in the 1950s and 1960s mostly in the cities of Arvada and Lakewood. By 1978, according to plan, the district declared 30 cottage units surplus and offered these units to other public agencies first. The Arvada Housing Authority acquired 19 units in the city (the Lakewood Housing Authority bought 10) and signed an agreement with a nonprofit housing corporation called Mountain United Church Housing Inc. (MUCH) to

rehabilitate and manage the units as low-income, large-family housing. Funding came from the Colorado Housing Finance Authority and Housing and Urban Development Section 8 Program.

A bitter political dispute arose in Arvada, because some residents feared and opposed subsidized housing projects in their neighborhoods. Two city council members, supporters of the scattered-site housing program, were targeted for a recall election, and heated public meetings were held. The political heat ended when the two council members won the recall election with a three to one vote of support. By 1980 the houses were occupied, the fight had subsided, and the remodeled ranch-

style brick homes with new sod and landscaping fit in with the other homes in the neighborhoods.

Contact: Joe Riedel
Assistant Superintendent
Dublin Schools
7030 Coffman Road
Dublin, Ohio 43017
(614) 761-5899

Edward Talbot, Manager
Housing and Community
Development Division
City of Arvada
8101 Ralston Road
Arvada, Colorado 80002
(303) 431-3020

*Scottish Corners
Elementary School in
Dublin, Ohio, is
designed in a
residential style and is
constructed to support
current and future
community uses.*

*Photo: Firestone Jaros
Mullin Architects*

Other Case Studies

COMMUNITY CENTERS

Terman School Center, Palo Alto, California

Current Use: Public open space and recreation, Jewish Community Center, and publicly assisted housing on 21.5 acres.

Original Use: Middle school including pool and playfields, built in 1955.

Description: The school facility, on seven acres of the site, is operated by the South Peninsula Jewish Community Center (JCC) and the city of Palo Alto. The Jewish Community Center operates the pool, gym, meeting rooms, and other facilities, all open to the public. The city operates a community center and library. The park and recreation fields, on 10.5 acres, are operated for the public by the city. The southwest four acres have been developed by the Palo Alto Housing Corporation (PAHC) into 85 moderate-income Section 8 housing units accommodating 235 people.

The complex is located on a major arterial near the Stanford Industrial Park, single-family housing, and a Veterans Administration hospital.

Palo Alto's Terman Middle School was typical of post–World War II institutional design—one-story buildings connected by utilitarian covered walkways. Note how the architects created warmth and texture by covering metal support pipes with redwood and breaking the visual monotony of low roofs with brightly colored banners overhead—two inexpensive solutions to conversion challenges.

Development Process: In 1978, the year Terman Middle School was closed, the school board appointed an advisory committee for the disposition of the site in accordance with requirements of the state education code. The committee met and established the following five priorities:

1. maintain all of the site for public recreation and community center use;

2. maintain a portion of the site as above with the remainder for private education, private recreation, or private community center use.

3. maintain a portion of the site for public uses as above, with the remainder for multifamily housing.

4. maintain a portion of the site for public use as above, with the remainder for single-family housing; and

5. use the entire site for private education, recreation, or community center purposes.

The school board voted to lease the site for the committee-defined uses. The Jewish Community Center and the Palo Alto Housing Corporation began to develop places for rent-assisted family housing. A neighborhood coalition also formed and opposed the JCC/PAHC plan in 1979, fearing loss of public access. In 1980 the city council adopted the concept of a community center and housing and directed city staff to create a

"Terman Working Group" comprising three neighborhood-elected delegates and appointed representatives from the city, JCC, and PAHC. The city hired a facilitator and budgeted an architect for the working group. In 1981, after a year's work, the Terman Working Group Plan was adopted by the city with the uses of open space, community center, and housing as described above.

Terms of the Deal: The city of Palo Alto has a lease purchase agreement with the school district for a 20-year period ending in the year 2001. The city made an initial payment of $1 million followed by annual payments of $450,000. Most of the building is sublet by the Jewish Community Center for yearly payments as shown:

Year 1 $137,300
Year 2 $146,911
Year 3 $157,195
Year 4 $168,198
Year 5 $179,972

Year 6 and after: Rental to increase by 65 percent of the increase in the San Francisco/Oakland Area consumer price index during the previous lease year

Further, the length of the sublease can be extended based on the value of leasehold improvements made in the first five years.

Within the first five years of lease term, improvements of

■ up to $1 million yield a
15-year lease,

■ between $1 million to $1.5 million yield a 20-year lease, and

■ in excess if $1.5 million yield a
25-year lease.

The Jewish Community Center has made leasehold improvements in excess of $1.5 million and therefore enjoys a 25-year lease.

Owner: City of Palo Alto
Department of Social and
Community Services
1305 Middlefield Road
Palo Alto, California 94301
Paul Thiltgen, Director
(415) 329-2239

Lessee: Albert Schultz Jewish
Community Center
655 Arastradero Road
Palo Alto, California 94306
Sandy Blovad, Executive Director
(415) 493-9400

Denver Indian Center, Denver, Colorado

Current Use: Multipurpose service center for Native Americans in the Denver metropolitan area and housing for the elderly and handicapped.

Original Use: A single-story brick elementary school, the Belmont School, built in the 1940s.

Description: The Denver Indian Center is located on a main arterial with mixed business and residential uses in a primarily Hispanic community in the southwestern portion of the city. The school building's redesign includes a facade with a Southwest Indian motif, new landscaping, parking improvements, and a fenced play area for preschoolers. The site totals seven acres, of which approximately half has been developed into 48 new units of HUD Section 202 housing for the elderly and handicapped. This housing faces away from the

main thoroughfare and is accessible from a residential street bordering the site.

The Indian Center serves a client base of 18,500 people through job training programs, adult education, youth services, and early childhood education. It has an annual budget of $1.6 million and 31 employees. The gymnasium/multipurpose room is available for cultural and social functions. Classroom space has been either converted to offices or retained for educational purposes.

Development Process: Belmont School was closed by the Denver Public School District in 1979 and sold to the Denver Housing Authority in 1980. The Housing Authority located its repair and maintenance operations in the building until 1983 when the Indian Center, which had lost its lease at a downtown site, moved in. A lease purchase agreement was developed whereby the Indian Center would lease the property for 10 years during which time Section 202 housing would be constructed, and the building would be renovated and used as a community service center. If these conditions were met, the Indian Center would own the building.

Conversion and rehabilitation funds were obtained from the Colorado Housing and Finance Authority and a city of Denver streetscape program. To undertake development of the HUD housing and to manage the building, the Indian Center formed the Denver Indian Center Development Corporation—a CDC. The development corporation joined forces with the Hispanic Denver Community Development Corporation (DCDC) to construct what has since become known as Belmont Housing on the former school playground site. The housing is managed by DCDC. With the completion of the housing project and building renovation, the Indian Center received title to the property in 1986.

Terms of the Deal: The school district sold the property outright for $388,000. The Denver Housing Authority leased the property to the Indian Center and created a performance lease, which could lead to purchase if the building were upgraded, the Indian population served, and Section 202 housing built. All parties received benefits from this arrangement.

Owner: Denver Indian Center
4407 Morrison Road
Denver, Colorado 80219
Wallace Coffey, Executive Director
(303) 936-2688

Sumner Hill House, Boston, Massachusetts

Current Use: Mixed-income rental housing.

Original Use: Jamaica Plain High School, built c. 1901.

Description: Designed in the Tudor Revival style and constructed of red brick and Indiana limestone, the four-story school is listed in the National Register of Historic Places. The architectural quality of the exterior was restored following the Secretary of the Interior's Standards for Rehabilitation and Guidelines ("accurately recovering the form and details of a property") and the interior renovated for 75 units of mixed-income rental housing. The renovation created 36 one-bedroom, 32 two-bedroom, and 7 three-bedroom apartments in a variety of layouts plus a community room; 54 parking spaces were also provided on an adjacent lot.

The building opened for occupancy in December 1986 and was immediately rented as a fully economically and racially integrated new housing community. The apartments are occupied by low-income (25 percent), moderate-income (50 percent), and higher income (25 percent) households; (see table, page 55). Building management and tenant selection is handled by Independent Managers, Inc., which maintains an on-site office and resident superintendent.

Development Process: Jamaica Plain High School was surplused when a new school was built. In the late 1970s, the city held an unsuccessful competition for developers. The school was slated at that time to be converted to condominiums. In 1984, a new city administration devised a strategy to pair a neighborhood development corporation with a private developer experienced in renovation and adaptive use. Complex financing was structured from state, local, and federal sources. Although integrated affordable housing based on a mixed-income rental

Sumner Hill House is mixed-income housing in the former Jamaica Plain High School. The beautifully restored school was built in 1901 and is listed in the National Register of Historic Places.

Photo: Keen Development Corp.

53

model met many of the city's goals, this prospect proved threatening to some of the adjacent residential property owners, who feared development of such a large project in their neighborhood.

To balance the many objectives for the school, the city sold the school for $1 to a special purpose entity—the Jamaica Plain Housing Trust, a partnership of the Sumner Hill Association and the Jamaica Plain Neighborhood Development Corporation. The trust was responsible for assuring that the renovations and operations satisfied neighborhood needs and concerns. The building was then leased to a local housing developer, Keen Development Corporation, which specializes in historic rehabilitation for affordable hous-

ing. A limited partnership was also created to raise equity utilizing the historic rehabilitation investment tax credits first contained in the Tax Reform Act of 1976. (These credits offered economic incentives for investors rehabilitating buildings listed in the National Register of Historic Places.). A profit-sharing agreement was also structured between the private developer and the Jamaica Plain Housing Trust.

Terms of the Deal: The $6.3 million renovation was financed with the following combination of funding sources:

■ $4.5 million mortgage loan from the Massachusetts Housing Finance Agency;

■ $530,000 Urban Development Action Grant (UDAG) from Department of Housing and Urban Development in the form of a loan through the city's Public Facilities Department;

■ $270,000 supplementary loan directly from the city of Boston;

The conversion and restoration of the Jamaica Plain High School was a joint undertaking between the Jamaica Plain Neighborhood Development Corporation and a private developer. The project has restored pride and confidence to a transitional neighborhood.

Photo: Keen Development Corp.

Sumner Hill House: 1989 Demographics				
	LOW INCOME	MODERATE INCOME	HIGHER INCOME	TOTAL	PERCENT
HOUSEHOLD TYPE					
Family	12	15	0	27	36
Elderly	0	1	0	1	1
Disabled	3	1	0	4	5
Single	5	18	20	43	58
Total	20	35	20	75	100
RACE/ETHNICITY					
White	4	22	12	38	51
Black	7	10	4	21	28
Hispanic	9	3	3	15	20
Asian	0	0	1	1	1
Native American	0	0	0	0	0
Total	20	35	20	75	100
PREVIOUS RESIDENCE					
Jamaica Plain	4	9	2	15	20
Boston	1	7	9	17	22
Greater Boston	14	19	5	38	51
Elsewhere	1	0	4	5	7
Total	20	35	20	75	100

Design features were protected, creating a unique environment for an unusual tenant mix—25% low income, 50% moderate income, and 25% higher income.

Photo: Keen Development Corp.

■ $2.3 million in private equity raised through a syndication of historic rehabilitation tax credit investors; and

■ 15-year rental assistance commitment from the executive office of Communities and Development under the innovative State Housing Assistance for Rental Production (SHARP) program.

After the 15 years of state rental subsidy, the building may be converted from rental to home ownership. However, residents will have first option to purchase their apartments at below-market prices. (Unfortunately, HUD backed out of its UDAG commitment, an action that is currently being challenged in court.)

Owner: Jamaica Plain Housing Trust
c/o Jamaica Plain Neighborhood
Development Corporation
31 Germania Street
Jamaica Plain, Massachusetts 02130
(617) 522-2424

Developer: Keen Development
Corporation (formerly
Housing Associates)
2 University Road, Box 2589
Cambridge, Massachusetts 02238
(617) 661-9100

Managers: Independent
Managers, Inc.
841 Parker Street
Boston, Massachusetts 02120
(617) 442-6828

Thomas Leen School, Dorchester, Massachusetts

Current Use: Congregate housing for mentally ill adults.

Original Use: Thomas Leen Elementary School, built 1926.

How Boston Designates a Developer for Special Needs Housing

Proposals are solicited by the city based on needs appropriate to the neighborhood as defined by planning and social service analyses and a feasibility study. The latter is typically done by Public Facilities Department staff. Once a responsive proposal has been tentatively selected, the Public Facilities Department project manager follows a nine-step process which leads to the purchase, sale, and closing of the surplus school property. These steps are:

1. Meet with elected officials from the affected community. If they do not oppose the proposed use, proceed to step 2.

2. Review proposal with mayor's office of neighborhood services. If they do not oppose, proceed to step 3.

3. Meet with neighborhood association leaders including the sub-planning and zoning advisory committees. (In Boston these committees are appointed by the elected Neighborhood Councils. The councils have advisory power regarding zoning ordinances.)

4. Schedule and hold meetings in the community where the proposer/developer makes a presentation and answers questions.

5. Respond to concerns and specifics raised in step 4 regarding the proposed use, developer, or process.

6. Solicit interested parties to form a Project Advisory Committee of 10 to 15 people. (In the case of Leen School, the Bailey Street neighborhood association was heavily involved.)

7. Gain project approval from the Public Facilities Commission and authorization to negotiate Tentative Developer Designation Agreement. The designation sets forth terms of the disposition of the property, its conversion uses, predevelopment timetable and preliminary development schedule. Upon successful completion of agreement, move to step 8.

8. Obtain Public Facilities Commission approval for final designation agreement. This is the development and construction agreement and also includes terms of future use, deed restrictions, etc.

9. Close sale just prior to construction when all financing and construction contractors are in place.

Development Process: The city's Public Facilities Department solicited proposals for either commercial or residential use. The proposal initially selected by the city was for a training center for the Glaziers and Asbestos Workers Union. This proposed use met with strong neighborhood opposition. Neighbors objected to the projected increases in traffic and the industrial nature of the training programs in an improving residential area. In the face of local opposition, the city designated another proposal, one from Mental Health Programs Inc. IV, to convert the school into 12 residential units for chronically mentally ill adults. The semi-independent living arrangement would include 24-hour staff. This proposal met with neighborhood approval and the city entered into a Tentative Developer Designation Agreement specifying conditions each party must meet to proceed with construction.

Terms of the Deal: The city will sell the property to the nonprofit developer for $1. Mental Health Programs Inc. agreed to obtain a Section 202 loan to adapt the school to a congregate care facility. All residents shall earn less than 80 percent of median income, and units shall be subsidized under HUD Section 8. Financing and design plans must meet with city approval. Should the developer change the use of the building within 50 years, the city has the option to purchase it.

Owners: Mental Health
Programs Inc. IV
28 Travis Street
Boston, Massachusetts 02134
(617) 254-7300

Ravenna School, Seattle, Washington

Current Use: Elderly housing and community center

Original Use: Ravenna Elementary School

Description: The brick school, built in 1911 with an addition in 1921, served a residential area until its closure in the early 1980s. The building has been converted to 39 apartments for low-income elderly residents. There are 34 one-bedroom units and 5 two-bedroom units. The units vary in size from 530 to 700 square feet. The Eckstein Community Center has been constructed on the site directly south of the school building. It is operated by the city Department of Parks and Recreation and contains a new gymnasium, locker rooms, and lobby, plus a kitchen, multipurpose area, and offices in part of the

Ravenna Elementary School circa 1915 served a residential neighborhood of Seattle. It was closed in the early 1980s.

Photo: Seattle Public School Archives

ground floor of the school building itself. One important feature of the joint use of the old school site is its intergenerational vitality, which has made this such a successful project.

Development Process: The school closure decision was fought by the surrounding community. Upon closing, the School Use Advisory Committee (SUAC) recommended that the site be used as a joint park and housing development. The voters of Seattle passed a $48 million

senior housing bond issue in 1981 to build 1,000 units of affordable housing for low-income elderly citizens. The city government accepted SUAC's recommendation and pressured the Seattle Housing Authority to convert Ravenna School under the Senior Housing Program. The housing authority initially balked at the particular site as it did not meet some of its location criteria: it was judged too hilly and too far from services. Today, however, Ravenna School Housing ranks as the most popular of all the Seattle Housing Authority's apartments.

Terms of the Deal: In 1984 the housing authority purchased the school building from the school district at the fair market value of $285,000. It then spent nearly $2 million in renovation and construction of the senior housing. Eligible tenants pay 27 percent of gross income for rent with a

Ravenna School converted to 39 apartments for low-income elderly [top] and augmented with construction of a new community center that plays off the original school's masonry design [middle]. Detail of design: the architects even designed a "sports-goyle" to adorn the outside of the community center. This one is a basketball.

Photos: ARC Architects

$100 per month minimum. A joint-use agreement permits the city Park and Recreation Department to own and manage the portion of the site that houses the community center. The city acquired this land from the school district for $680,000 and spent an additional $1.3 million constructing the center.

Owner: Seattle Housing Authority
126 Sixth Avenue North
Seattle, Washington 98109
Fred Kay, Director, Maintenance and Construction
(206) 443-4425

Rotary Manor, San Rafael, California

Current Use: Apartments for the elderly.

Original Use: West End Elementary School, built in 1926.

Description: The four-acre site is situated in a residential area close to shopping and city services. The original school building now contains 15 housing units—4 single-room apartments with patios, 6 one-bedroom units, 5 handicapped units, and 1 recreation room. Two new 24-unit apartment buildings of three stories each were built on site in 1982, and 36 more apartments were added in 1986. A total of 99 elderly units occupy the landscaped site. There are 107 residents, 101 widows, and 3 married couples. The average age is 76, and the average income is $10,000.

Development Process: The San Rafael Rotary Club sought a community project in 1978 and looked at the possibility of building housing for the many low- and moderate-income elderly residents of Marin County who were being priced out of the community because of dramatic increases in property values. The 175-member Rotary Club took on the project, looked for land on which to build, and found the West End School. The city of San Rafael agreed to purchase the property from the school district for $595,000 and sell it for $1 to a nonprofit corporation established for the project named the Rotary Manor Corporation. Rotary Manor Corporation raised $80,000 for preliminary planning and obtained private financing for the project. However, plans were put on hold for two years, because interest rates reached 20 percent and made the project infeasible. Development resumed when a private foundation offered financing at 8 percent. With a combination of contributions of time and labor from Rotarians, construction commenced and was completed by 1982.

Residents of Rotary Manor must be over 62 years of age, meet Department of Housing and Urban Development low- and moderate-income guidelines, must have lived in Marin County for the previous five years, and cannot be members of the local Rotary Club. The facility is intended for independent living, and each resident is required to have a "sponsor," a family member, or a friend who will assist in times of ill health. The facility is owned and administered by the Rotary Manor Corp., which hires resident managers.

Terms of the Deal: Phases 1 and 2 cost about $1.5 million each. Funds were borrowed privately and are repaid from rental income. Contributions of materials and labor have resulted in construction costs of less than half the prevailing market figures. Rents for the 600-square-foot apartments are $325 per month compared to the average comparable rent of $1,100 per month in Marin County. The fully occupied complex has a $300 per month positive cash flow without any public operating subsidy.

Owner: Rotary Manor Corporation
1821 Fifth Avenue
San Rafael, California 94901
Jock McNutt, President
(415) 459-6558

Rotary Manor. Starting with the closed West End Elementary School, the San Rafael Rotary Club renovated classrooms into 15 housing units for low-income elderly residents and then built 84 new units on the site.

Abrahams School, Roslindale, Massachusetts

Current Use: Headquarters and training center of International Brotherhood of Painters and Allied Trades.

Original Use: Henry Abrahams Elementary School, built in the late 1920s.

Description: A relatively small structure of 16,000 square feet, the school's 10 classrooms were mostly vacant from 1981 to 1989. The building sits on a 41,000-square-foot lot surrounded by what are known in Boston as triple deckers (three-story multifamily residences) and by light industry. One side of the site is zoned light manufacturing and industrial, the other side is zoned multifamily residential. The new addition of 12,000 square feet was constructed on stilts and provides modern office space as well as protected parking below, an important factor for workers who carry their tools of the trade with them in their cars.

Development Process: The International Brotherhood of Painters and Allied Trades was seeking a new facility for its offices and training programs. For historical reasons the union had always been located in Boston, and for practical reasons, since the city of Boston requires that construction projects employ 50 percent Boston residents, the union wanted to stay in Boston. An old school was considered suitable for a training facility, and the Thomas Leen School in Dorchester seemed a good candidate. However, neighbor-

hood opposition (see page 57) scuttled that plan. The city's Public Facilities Department selected the Abrahams site as an alternative knowing that the zoning, site, and neighborhood composition would more likely welcome the new use. No RFP was issued, rather a direct designation was made.

Terms of the Deal: The city sold the building for $1. In return Boston received a $3 million investment in a poorer neighborhood, retention of a major trade union, and a new training center geographically located where jobs are needed. Through deed restrictions, the city is requiring that the union notify the surrounding community of any pre-apprenticeship programs and jobs, that the facility have open houses, that presentations about opportunities in the trades be made in local high schools, and that a meeting room be available for community use. Construction financing is provided entirely by the owner.

Owners: International Brotherhood of Painters and Allied Trades
20 Mahler Road
Roslindale, Massachusetts 02134
(617) 731-6800

Printing and Binding Facility, Arlington, Virginia

Current Use: Printing, binding, collating, mailing, and specialty handwork facility for persons with mental illness and developmental disabilities.

Original Use: Nelly Custis School, built in 1929, with additions in 1957 and 1965.

Description: A brick building of one and two stories in a mixed residential and commercial area of Arlington, Virginia, it houses complete print facilities, warehouse, custom packaging, and collating sheltered workshop. The facility employs 70 workers and 15 staff.

Development Process: The school was closed in 1980, one of eight schools closed by the Arlington County School District. The Sheltered Occupational Center (SOC) owned a 6,800-square-foot printing facility in nearby Ballston at the time but was looking for a larger space. Arlington County was looking for land near the new subway station in Ballston, an area that had just been rezoned from industrial and commercial to office and residential uses. SOC's facility was now out of compliance with existing zoning, and the county real estate office proposed to trade SOC's site for the 38,000-square-foot Custis site.

It turned out to be a win-win situation for both parties. SOC had searched for commercial and industrial property near the Washington, D.C., area and could not find affordable property. The closed schools they had examined were not zoned properly. Fortuitously, the Custis School site was zoned for commercial use and was served by public transit. The county worked with the school district to transfer title to SOC. A use permit was obtained and must be renewed every five years because of the printing and storage activities on site.

Neighborhood fears of mentally re-
tarded persons or of a noisy industrial neighbor have been offset by a
quiet, well-maintained physical plant
and continuance of the old school's
use as a polling place. At the most
recent reuse permit hearing, no
neighborhood complaints were
voiced at all.

Terms of the Deal: SOC relinquished
title to its Ballston property to
Arlington County in exchange for
the Custis School, use permit, and
$350,000 in federal Community De-
velopment Block Grant funds for
renovation. SOC contributed
$200,000 for renovation. The county
retained a small portion of the site as
a mini-park and buffer between the
sheltered workshop and the adjoining neighbors. In 1983 SOC moved
into the Custis School and inherited
a day care center that had been leasing space in the facility as a tenant,
an arrangement continued until
1988.

Owner: Sheltered Occupational
Center of Northern Virginia
750 South 23rd Street
Arlington, Virginia 22202
Richard Valentine, President
(703) 920-9400

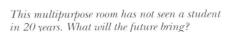

*This multipurpose room has not seen a student
in 20 years. What will the future bring?*

Contacts

For further information about any of the projects discussed here, the following contacts are listed alphabetically by city:

Albuquerque, New Mexico
Albuquerque High School
Contact: Victoria Prinz, Planner
Redevelopment and Planning
Department
City of Albuquerque
P.O. Box 1293
Albuquerque, New Mexico 87103
(505) 768-3283

Arlington, Virginia
Printing and Binding Facility
Owner: Sheltered Occupational
Center of Northern Virginia
750 South 23rd Street
Arlington, Virginia 22202
Richard Valentine, President
(703) 920-9400

Arvada, Colorado
Cottage Schools Housing
Manager: Edward Talbot,
Housing and Community
Development Division
City of Arvada
8101 Ralston Road
Arvada, Colorado 80002
(303) 431-3020

Boston, Massachusetts
Abrahams School
Owners: International Brotherhood
of Painters and Allied Trades
20 Mahler Road
Roslindale, Massachusetts 02134
(617) 731-6800

Bowditch School
Owner: Bowditch School Limited
Partnership
Managers: Paul Sullivan,
Housing Trust
434 Harrison Avenue
Boston, Massachusetts 02118
Mark Baker, Director
(617) 574-9004

Sumner Hill House
Owner: Jamaica Plain Housing Trust
c/o Jamaica Plain Neighborhood
Development Corporation
31 Germania Street
Jamaica Plain, Massachusetts 02130
(617) 522-2424

Developer: Keen Development
Corporation (formerly Housing
Associates)
2 University Road, Box 2589
Cambridge, Massachusetts 02238
(617) 661-9100

Managers: Independent
Managers, Inc.
841 Parker Street
Boston, Massachusetts 02120
(617) 442-6828

Thomas Leen School
Owners: Mental Health
Programs Inc. IV
28 Travis Street
Boston, Massachusetts 02134
(617) 254-7300

Cleveland, Ohio
The Hodge School
Owner: The St. Clair Superior
Coalition
6408 St. Clair Avenue
Cleveland, Ohio 44103
(216) 881-0644
Renee Berry, Executive Director

Development Consultant:
Shorebank Advisory Services
1950 East 71st Street
Chicago, Illinois 60649
(312) 288-0066

Denver, Colorado
Capitol Hill Senior Resource Center
Owner: Capitol Hill Senior
Resources, Inc.
1420 Ogden Street
Denver, Colorado 80218
(303) 832-8731

Denver Indian Center
Owner: Denver Indian Center
4407 Morrison Road
Denver, Colorado 80219
Wallace Coffey, Executive Director
(303) 936-268

Dublin, Ohio
**New Construction with
Conversion in Mind**
Contact: Joe Riedel,
Assistant Superintendent
Dublin Schools
7030 Coffman Road
Dublin, Ohio 43017
(614) 761-5899

Dunn, North Carolina
**Triangle South Mall
Business Enterprise Center**
Manager: Triangle South
Enterprise Center
600 South Magnolia Avenue
Dunn, North Carolina 28334
Nancy Blackman, Executive Director
(919) 892-8775

East Palo Alto, California
Ravenswood High School
Contacts: Linda Hamilton-Rahi,
Deputy City Manager
City of East Palo Alto
2415 University Avenue
East Palo Alto, California 94303
(415) 853-3100

Sherrill Houghton,
Assistant Superintendent
Administrative Services
Sequoia Union High School District
480 James Avenue
Redwood City, California 94062
(415) 369-1411, Extension 217

Gully, Minnesota
Gully Center
Contact: Leona Humphrey,
Department of Trade and
Economic Development
900 American Center Building
150 East Kellogg Boulevard
St. Paul, Minnesota 55101
(612) 296-5005

Palo Alto, California
Terman School Center
Owners: City of Palo Alto
Department of Social and
Community Services
1305 Middlefield Road
Palo Alto, California 94301
Paul Thiltgen, Director
(415) 329-2239

Lessee: Albert Schultz Jewish
Community Center
655 Arastradero Road
Palo Alto, California 94306
Sandy Blovad, Executive Director
(415) 493-9400

Port Costa, California
Port Costa Elementary School
Owner: Port Costa
Conservation Society
P.O. Box 36
Port Costa, California 94569
Mary Powell, Development Officer
(415) 787-2880

San Bruno, California
Pen/Crest Center
Owner: San Mateo Union High
School District
650 North Delaware Street
San Mateo, California 94401
John Mahaffy, Director of Fiscal
Services
(415) 348-8834

Contact: Kathy McNeil
Pen/Crest Center Rentals
and Leases
300 Piedmont Avenue
San Bruno, California 94066
(415) 583-4293

San Francisco, California
Farragut School Site
Owner: San Francisco Unified
School District
Property Management Department
801 Toland Street
San Francisco, California 94124
Lawrence Jacobsen, Manager
(415) 695-2356

**San Francisco Center/
Fifth and Market**
Owner: San Francisco Unified
School District
Property Management Department
801 Toland Street
San Francisco, California 94124
Lawrence Jacobsen, Manager
(415) 695-2356

San Rafael, California
Rotary Manor
Owner: Rotary Manor Corporation
1821 Fifth Avenue
San Rafael, California 94901
Jock McNutt, President
(415) 459-6558

Sunnyvale, California
Westinghouse Engineering Center
Owner: Assistant Superintendent
for Business
Fremont Union High School District
589 Fremont
Sunnyvale, California 94087
Mike Raffetto
(408) 522-2210

Lessee: Westinghouse Marine
Division Engineering Center
401 East Hendy Avenue
P.O. Box 3499
Sunnyvale, California 94088
Frank Rodrigues, Facilities Manager
(408) 735-2608

Scottsdale, Arizona
Scottsdale High School
Contact: Robert C. Hubley,
Assistant Superintendent of Business
Services
Scottsdale Public Schools
P.O. Box 15428
Phoenix, Arizona 85060
(602) 952-6144

Seattle, Washington
Oak Tree Village
Owner: Seattle Public Schools
Facilities Department
4141 Fourth Avenue South
Seattle, Washington 98134
John Richmond, Manager
(206) 298-7630

Ravenna School
Owner: Seattle Housing Authority
126 Sixth Avenue North
Seattle, Washington 98109
Fred Kay, Director
Maintenance and Construction
(206) 443-4425

Wallingford Center
Owners: Lorig Associates
2001 Western Avenue
Seattle, Washington 98101
(206) 728-7660

Seattle Public Schools
Facilities Department
4141 Fourth Avenue South
Seattle, Washington 98134
John Richmond, Manager
(206) 298-7630

Washington, D.C.
Sumner and Magruder Schools
Owner: District of Columbia
Schools; Sumner School Museum
and Archives
17th & M Streets NW
Washington, D.C. 20036
Richard Hurlbut, Director
(202) 646-7600

Bibliography

Adaptive Reuse of School Buildings: A Bibliography. Mary Ellen Huls. 1985. Vance Bibliographies, P.O. Box 229, Monticello, Illinois 61856.

Adaptive Reuse of School Buildings: A Selective and Annotated Bibliography No. 182. Jacqueline Snider. 1986. Council of Planning Librarians, Chicago, Illinois.

Surplus School Space: Options and Opportunities. 1976. Educational Facilities Laboratories, New York.

Community School Centers. 1979. Educational Facilities Laboratories, New York.

Surplus Schools. Information Sheet No. 32. Holly Fiala. 1982. National Trust for Historic Preservation, Washington, D.C.

A Guide for the Adaptive Use of Surplus Schools. Jack W. Giljahn and Thomas R. Matheny. 1981. Columbus Landmarks Foundation, Columbus, Ohio.

Surplus School Space—the Problem and the Possibilities. 1978. Council of Educational Facilities Planners International, Columbus, Ohio.

School Building Reuse Case Studies. 1981. Executive Office of Communities and Development, Commonwealth of Massachusetts, Boston, Massachusetts.

Establishing a School Building Reuse Process. 1981. Executive Office of Communities and Development, Commonwealth of Massachusetts, Boston, Massachusetts.

The Surplus School Site: Problem or Opportunity. 1983. Citizens League of Marin, San Rafael, California.

Adaptive Reuse for Elderly Housing: Guidebook for Mayors and Local Officials. 1986. U.S. Conference of Mayors, Washington, D.C.

Index

For ease of access, examples of school conversions are grouped by categories with page numbers.

The three categories are:

■ New use

■ Location

■ Financing and development methods

New Use

Community Centers and Social Services

Denver Indian Center, Denver, CO, 52

Capitol Hill Senior Resources, Denver, CO, 30

Business and Professional Offices

Westinghouse Marine Engineering Center, Sunnyvale, CA, 40

Triangle South Enterprise Center, Dunn, NC, 44

17th and M Offices / Sumner School Museum, Washington, DC, 41

Sheltered Occupational Workshop, Arlington, VA, 60

Painters and Allied Trades Union, Boston, MA, 60

Mixed Use

Community Center/Housing
Terman School, Palo Alto, CA, 51

Pen/Crest Center,
San Bruno, CA, 21

Serramonte High School,
Daly City, CA, 17

Wallingford Center,
Seattle, WA, 31

Housing

Hodge School, Cleveland, O, 23

Cottage Schools, Arvada, CO, 49

Sumner Hill House, Boston, MA, 53

Ravenna School, Seattle, WA, 57

Rotary Manor, San Rafael, CA, 59

Thomas Leen School,
Boston, MA, 56

Bowditch School, Boston, MA, 26

Retail/Malls

San Francisco Centre,
San Francisco, CA, 38

Oak Tree Village, Seattle, WA, 39

Scottsdale High School,
Scottsdale, AZ, 34

Historic Preservation

Albuquerque High School,
Albuquerque, NM, 36

Bowditch School, Boston, MA, 26

Jamaica Plain High School,
Boston, MA, 53

Port Costa School,
Port Costa, CA, 45

Sumner School, Washington, DC, 41

Wallingford Center Seattle, WA, 31

Location

Big City
(over 400,000 pop.)

Boston, MA, 13, 26, 40, 53, 56, 60

Cleveland, OH, 11, 23

Denver, CO, 30, 52

San Francisco, CA, 33, 38

Seattle, WA, 12, 15, 31, 39, 57

Washington, DC, 12, 41

Medium City
(under 200,000 pop.)

Albuquerque, NM, 36,

Arlington, VA, 60

Arvada, CO, 49

Daly City, CA, 17

Dublin, OH, 49

East Palo Alto, CA, 33

Palo Alto, CA, 11, 13, 51

San Bruno, CA, 21

San Rafael, CA, 59

Scottsdale, AZ, 34

Sunnyvale, CA, 40

Small Town
(under 10,000 pop.)

Dunn, NC, 44

Gully, MN, 48

Port Costa, CA, 45

Photo: Mary Levin

Daniel Carlson is a research consultant at the Institute for Public Policy
and Management, Graduate School
of Public Affairs, University of Washington. He received a masters of city
and regional planning from the University of California, Berkeley, and
his undergraduate degree in government from Oberlin College. He
works with nonprofit and public organizations to enhance the built environment and steward the natural
environment and is the author of
many studies and reports ranging
from school facilities plans to how to
protect Puget Sound. Carlson draws
on experience as a mayoral aid,
foundation director, and community
development planner in approach-
ing his work. This book , his first, offers examples of how public, private,
and nonprofit organizations inter-re-
late to build sustainable communities. Dan is married and lives with his
wife and two children on a small
farm on an island in Puget Sound.